FLORENCE

A COMPLETE GUIDE FOR VISITING THE CITY

ALL THE MUSEUMS,
THE CHURCHES
AND THE GALLERIES
INCLUDED THE RESTORED
WORKS OF ART

LARGE MONUMENTAL PLAN
WITH THE ROAD-MAP
AND USEFUL INFORMATION

BONECHI

View of Florence

Brief historical survey The river Arno cuts its way through the broad plain on which Florence lies, surrounded by the out-hills of the Tusco-Emilian Appennines. Already occupied in prehistoric times, as early as the 8th century B.C. an Italic peoples with a Villanovan culture settled in the area between the Arno and Mugnone rivers, but little is known of these remote times. In 57 B.C. the Roman city was founded with the square ground plan of the *castrum*. The *decumanus* was laid out along what are now the Via del Corso, the Via degli Speziali and the Via Strozzi, while the ancient *cardus* corresponds to the line between Piazza San Giovanni, the Via Roma and the Via Calimala. Marcus Aurelius (or it may have been Diocletian) chose it as the seat of the *Corrector Italiae*, or governor responsible for Tuscany and Umbria. With the arrival of the barbarians, Florence was first besieged by the Ostrogoths (405) of Radagaisus, who plundered the surrounding countryside,

although Florence managed to resist and Stilicho's troops inflicted an overwhelming defeat on the enemy. Next came the Byzantines, who occupied Florence in 539, and the Goths who took over the city in 541. Under Lombard domination (570) it managed to safeguard its autonomy, while under the Franks the number of inhabitants diminished and the city lost most of its territory. Around the year thousand things began to change for the better and the "lily" city's rise continued for various centuries in spite of numerous controversies, wars and internecine struggles.

New walls surrounded the city, new civic and religious buildings went up, and at the same time the arts, literature, and trade continued to prosper. In 1183 the city became a free commune, even though it had already actually availed itself of this freedom for many years. The first clashes between the two factions, Guelph and Ghibelline, date to those years. The former were followers of the Pope, the latter of the Emperor. The ensuing struggles were to lacerate the civic fabric of the city up to 1268.

No holds were barred in the civic struggle. The Ghibellines were the first to have the upper hand and expelled the Guelph families from the city in 1249. But Florence was basically Guelph and the next year victory fell to their lot. The Ghibellines sought refuge in Siena where they were overtaken by the Guelph troops, who were, however, badly beaten in the battle of Monteaperti. As a result Florence was once more Ghibelline for various years until the battle of Benevento (1226), when the Guelphs once more got the upper hand and defeated their bitter rivals once and for all.

Despite the unstable social and political situation, this period witnessed an upsurge in the arts and in literature. This was the time of Dante and the «dolce stil novo», of Giotto and Arnolfo di Cambio.

In the 15th century the city's rise continued. Florence was a trading city but also the new cradle for Italian and eventually European culture. Many powerful families (the Pitti, Frescobaldi, Strozzi, Albizi) vied for supremacy in the city. One above all soon came to the fore, a powerful family of bankers - the Medici - and beginning with the founder Cosimo I, later known as the Elder, they were to govern up to the first half of the 18th century, transforming Florence into a beacon during the period of Humanism and the Renaissance. Great personalities such as Leonardo da Vinci and Michelangelo characterized the period and Florentine prestige reached its zenith.

In 1737 the Medicis gave way to the house of Lorraine and the government continued along the lines of a moderate liberalism even if at that point the great period of Florentine culture was on the wane. In 1860, during the Risorgimento, Tuscany was annexed to the Realm of Italy with a plebiscite. For a brief period Florence then became the capital of the new nation.

During World War II serious damage was inflicted on the historical center and various important buildings were irremediably lost. Despite this and despite the flood which raged through the city in 1966, Florence has retained its charm.

AREA OF

THE DUOMO

Baptistery of San Giovanni - Duomo - Giotto's Campanile - Museo dell'Opera del Duomo - Loggia del Bigallo - Museo della Loggia del Bigallo

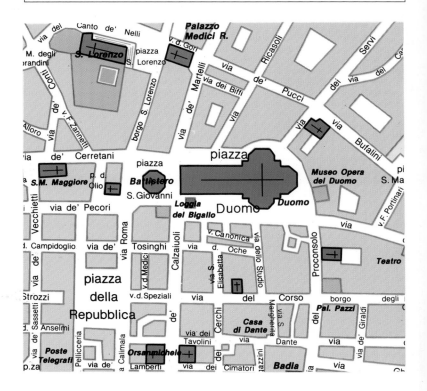

Baptistery The Florentine Baptistery seems originally to have been built around the 4th-5th century in an area occupied by a large Roman *domus* and its peripheral parts extended as far as the area later occupied by Santa Reparata. The site was near the north gate of Roman Florence (brought to light between the Baptistery and the Via Cerretani), and the religious building was from the beginning octagonal in plan with a semi-circular apse and was set on a stepped podium.

In the 11th century the Baptistery became the city cathedral since Santa Reparata was being rebuilt. San Giovanni (the Baptistery) too was refaced both inside and out, while in 1128 the smooth pyramidal roof was finished and topped by a lantern with columns (1150).

The *apse* - also called *Scarsella* - was rebuilt in a square shape in 1292 and in 1293, when the work done at the behest of the Arte di Calimala (wool merchants' guild) was finished, the Baptistery looked as it does today. The building where the Florentine Republic invested its knights is still today faced on the **exterior** by green and white marble. Each side is divided into three areas by pilaster strips which support an entablature below and round arches with windows above. The uppermost entablature has an attic subdivided into blind compartments.

The three bronze **doors** are particularly important. The *South door*, which is the oldest and which is decorated with scenes from the *Life of St. John the Baptist* and the *Allegories of the Theologian and Cardinal Virtues*, is by Andrea Pisano (1330-1336).

Baptistery

The *North door* with *Stories from the New Testament, Evangelists and Doctors of the Church* is by Lorenzo Ghiberti (1403-1424), with the help of Donatello, Bernardo Ciuffagni, Paolo Uccello and Bernardo Cennini. And lastly the *Eastern door* known as the «*Gates of Paradise*» with ten panels (now replaced by copies) which represent *Stories from the Old Testament*. The work of Lorenzo Ghiberti, this ensemble is one of the greatest masterpieces of 15th-century sculpture.

The **interior** has an inlaid pavement with decorative motives of eastern derivation. On the walls from left to right: a Roman *sarcophagus*, the *sarcophagus of Bishop Ranieri* and the *tomb of Baldassare Coscia, the Antipope John XIII* (1427), designed by Michelozzo and Donatello, who executed the reclining statue. The Baptistery also houses a marble *baptismal font* of 1371, attributed to the school of Pisa.

The tribune in the apse has Byzantine style *mosaics* on the vault done around 1225 by Fra Jacopo. Other mosaics cover the entire **cupola**, at which Florentine artists possibly aided by Venetian craftsmen worked between the 13th and the 14th centuries. These artists included Cimabue, Coppo di Marcovaldo and Gaddo Gaddi.

The tondo above the apse represents *Christ* surrounded by scenes of the *Last Judgement*. The opposite side contains *Stories of the Baptist*, scenes from the *Life of Christ*, and from the *Life of Joseph and Mary* as well as *Stories from Genesis*. The *Angelic Hierarchies* are represented around the lantern.

Baptistery: Gates of Paradise and details

GATES OF PARADISE:
Episodes from the old testament depicted in the ten panels.

Creation of Adam and Eve. The Fall. The Expulsion from Paradise.	*Work of the first men. Sacrifice of Cain and Abel. Cain kills Abel. God reproves Cain.*
Noah and his family offering sacrifice after having left the ark. Drunkenness of Noah.	*The Angels appear to Abraham. Sacrifice of Isaac.*
Birth of Esau and Jacob. Sale of the birthright of the first-born. Isaac orders Esau to go hunting. Esau out hunting. Rebekah counsels Jacob. Isaac is deceived.	*Joseph sold to the merchants. Discovery of the cup of gold in Benjamin's sack. Joseph reveals himself to his brothers.*
On Mount Sinai Moses receives the Tables of the Law.	*The people of Israel in the River Jordan. The Fall of Jericho.*
Battle against the Philistines. David kills Goliath.	*Solomon receives the Queen of Sheba.*

Gates of Paradise At present Ghiberti's famous doors are being restored. The action of rain and smog have covered the splendid reliefs with an opaque patina. The pictures show us the doors as they originally appeared before these corrosive agents set to work and permit us to appreciate fully their exquisite beauty. The all-over view is followed by details of the heads of Lorenzo Ghiberti and his son Vittorio, tondos which, with other portraits of contemporary artists, decorate the frame of the doors.

Baptistery: interior and dome

Duomo or Cathedral of Santa Maria del Fiore

Duomo The Duomo or Cathedral of Florence, dedicated to Santa Maria del Fiore, is the fruit of the commitment of a large number of artists who worked on it over a period of centuries.

At the end of the 13th century communal Florence was already flourishing and its urban fabric had spread considerably. The extant cathedral of Santa Reparata was by now too small to house the citizens and was no longer sufficiently prestigious for the city. In his *Cronache* Giovanni Villani narrates that «the citizens came to an agreement on the renewal of the principal church of Florence, which was of a simple form and small in comparison to a city of this kind; and they gave orders to make it larger and set the facade further back, and to make it all in marble and with sculptured figures».

In 1294 the Corporazione delle Arti (Guilds), upon which the government was based, decreed that Arnolfo di Cambio should construct a new cathedral and that, when the building was completed, the preexisting church be torn down.

At the time *Santa Reparata* was situated where the front part of the cathedral now stands.

The Church had been built in the 4th-5th centuries on the ruins of a Roman *domus*, and it was tripartite with a single apse. At the time of the Byzantine wars the church was destroyed and then rebuilt between the 8th and 9th centuries. Although the perimeter was basically the same, two side chapels were added to the structure and the columns were replaced by piers with pilaster strips. Between the year 1000 and 1100 a crypt with a raised choir was created in the area of the apse, which was flanked by two bell towers outside. The new cathedral construction yard grew around and inside this church and

Duomo: Brunelleschi's dome

even though it lasted for decades, the life of Santa Reparata was maintained intact until 1375. Work on the new cathedral, begun on Sept. 8, 1296, was interrupted in 1302 with the death of Arnolfo di Cambio, whose place as *capomastro* or overseer was taken by Giotto in 1334. Even so the social situation and various natural calamities (the economic crisis due to the crash of the Bardi and Peruzzi banks, the flood of 1333, the popular uprisings and the plague of 1348) slowed up construction.

After Giotto's death in 1337, Andrea Pisano, Francesco Talenti and Giovanni di Lapo Ghini worked on the Duomo. In 1375 Santa Reparata was demolished to the height of two and a half meters and the plans for the cathedral were changed so that part of Arnolfo's structure was torn down. The building was finally finished with the exception of the dome, which had been included in the original project but turned out to be more difficult to build than planned. The competition for the dome was won in 1420 by Brunelleschi, who proposed to build the enormous aerial structure without the use of fixed centering thanks to the adoption of interconnected ribbing and interlocking herringbone courses of bricks. The dome was terminated in 1434 and the cathedral was consecrated in 1436, 140 years after it had been begun.

The lantern at the top of the dome was also designed by Brunelleschi, but as Vasari notes «Because he was now old and would not live to see the lantern finished he stipulated in his will that it should be built with the model and the written instructions that he left; otherwise, he insisted, the fabric would collapse because it was vaulted in an ogive and needed the weight pressing down on top in order to strengthen it. He failed to see this edifice

11

The Cathedral of Florence

completed before he died, but he raised it to a height of several feet...».
Arnolfo's **facade** was torn down in 1587 and designs for a new one abound-
ed. Not until 1871 were the plans by De Fabris approved and they were then
carried out in 1887. This facade, which is the one we now see, employed
the same types of marble as those used in the revestment of the sides: Car-
rara white, Prato green and Maremma rose. Above the three portals with
Stories from the Life of the Virgin are three lunettes with, left to right, *Charity*,
the *Madonna with the Patrons of the City*, and *Faith*. The gable of the main
entrance has a *Madonna in Glory*. Statues of the *Apostles* and of the *Virgin*
form the frieze between the rose windows at the side and the one in the
center. The tympanum with a bas-relief of *God the Father* is set above a row
of busts of artists.

Duomo: Dante and the Divine Comedy, *Domenico di Michelino*

Duomo: John Hawkwood, *Paolo Uccello;*
Niccolò da Tolentino, *Andrea del Castagno.*

Four doors open in the sides of the cathedral which is articulated by pilasters
and tall two-light windows. On the side of the campanile is the *Porta del Campanile* and the *Porta dei Canonici* while on the other side are the *Porta della
Balla* and the *Porta della Mandorla.* The «*Mandorla*» is 15th century and is
decorated in the lunette with a mosaic of the *Annunciation* by Ghirlandaio,
a tympanum by Nanni di Banco, and statues of the *Prophets* by the young
Donatello.
In the *interior* there is a strong feeling for space, both vertical and horizontal, in keeping with the dictates of Italian Gothic architecture. The three
broad aisles are divided by composite piers from which spring large mode-
rately pointed arches. The spaciousness of the bays unifies the area of the
cathedral, enhacing its width. The aisles flow into the area of the high altar
around which the three apses or tribunes, each divided into five rooms,
radiate.
Under the stained glass designed by Ghiberti and Paolo Uccello's *Clock*
(1443), the *interior facade* bears the 14th-century lunette with the *Coronation of the Virgin* by Gaddo Gaddi, and the *tomb of Antonio d'Orso*, by Tino
di Camaino, around 1321.
The *left aisle* is only apparently unadorned for it contains various masterpieces of art: at the beginning is the edicule with a statue of *Joshua*, by
Ciuffagni, Donatello and Nanni di Bartolo, and the neighboring *edicule of S.
Zanobius* painted at the end of the 14th century by Vanni del Biondo. Between Benedetto da Maiano's *bust of A. Squarcialupi* and Ciuffagni's *edicule
with David* (1434) are the two *equestrian monuments*, frescoes now detached
from the wall, of *Giovanni Acuto* (John Hawkwood) and *Niccolò da Tolentino.*
The former was painted by Paolo Uccello in 1436 and represents the soldier
of fortune with a severity that borders on immobility while in the latter (1456)
Andreà del Castagno's livelier plasticity bestows a sense of animation on the
knight.
In front of the arch of the fouth bay, under the *stained-glass window* designed
by Agnolo Gaddi, are the panels with *SS. Cosmas and Damian* (by Bicci di
Lorenzo, 15th cent.) and *Dante Alighieri* (by Domenico di Michelino, 1465).
The left tribune, besides Lorenzo di Credi's *St. Joseph* in the first room on
the left, once contained Michelangelo's marble *Pietà* which is now in the
nearby Museo dell'Opera del Duomo.
Two marble edicules flank the door of the *Sacrestia Nuova* (New Sacristy)
with a lunette in glazed terra cotta by Luca della Robbia. This *Resurrection*
which Luca made in 1444 is enhanced by an ascending movement that is
both linear and sculptural, and is enriched by color. On the opposite side,
beyond the *high altar* - a 16th-century work by Baccio Bandinelli - there is,

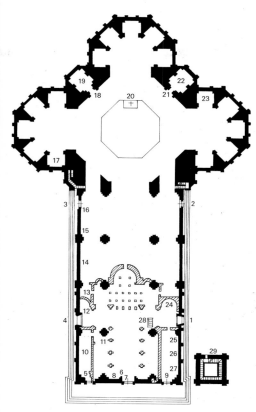

DUOMO

1) Porta del Campanile
2) Porta dei Canonici
3) Porta della Mandorla
4) Porta della Balla
5) Stained-glass window with St. Stephen (cartoon by L. Ghiberti)
6) Stained-glass window with the Assumption (cartoon by L. Ghiberti)
7) Coronation of the Virgin (Gaddo Gaddi)
8) Tomb of Bishop Antonio d'Orso (Tino di Camaino)
9) Stained-gloss window with St. Lawrence (cartoon by L. Ghiberti)
10) Statue of Joshua (Ciuffagni, Donatello, Nanni di Bartolo)
11) Edicule of St. Zanobius (Giovanni del Biondo)
12) Bust of A. Squarcialupi (Benedetto da Maiano)
13) Equestrian monument to Niccolò da Tolentino (Andrea del Castagno)
14) Equestrian monument to John Hawkwood (Paolo Uccello)
15) Saints Cosmas and Damian (Bicci di Lorenzo)
16) Dante and the Divine Comedy (Domenico di Michelino)
17) St. Joseph (Lorenzo di Credi)
18) Resurrection (Luca della Robbia)
19) Sacrestia Nuova or delle Messe
20) High Altar (Baccio Bandinelli)
21) Ascension (Luca della Robbia)
22) Sacrestia Vecchia or dei Canonici
23) "Madonna del Popolo" (fresco, school of Giotto)
24) St. Bartholomew Enthroned (Rossello di Jacopo Franchi)
25) Half figure of Giotto (Benedetto da Maiano)
26) Statue of a Prophet (Nanni di Banco)
27) Bust of Brunelleschi (Buggiano)
28) Entrance to the Crypt of Santa Reparata
29) Giotto's Campanile

Duomo: interior and the remains of Santa Reparata

in mirror image, the door ot the **Sacrestia Vecchia** (Old Sacristy) with Luca della Robbia's other lunette of the *Ascension*. The right tribune contains a Giottesque fresco with the *Madonna* and a *St. Philip* by Bandini. Beyond this in the south aisle is a painting of *St. Bartholomew Enthroned* by Franchi (15th cent.) and the edicule with a *Prophet* by Nanni di Banco (1408), set between a *roundel* of Giotto (by Benedetto da Maiano, 1490) and a bust of Brunelleschi (by Buggiano, 1446). Here a modern staircase descends to the pre-existant church of Santa Reparata.

The great **dome**, which Brunelleschi had conceived as bare, was however painted by Giorgio Vasari and Zuccari between 1572 and 1579. Scenes from the *Last Judgement* are set in three concentric bands with the *Prophets* at the top of the vault in a *trompe l'oeil* lantern with a railing. A passageway let into the thickness of the dome leads to the frescoes and, from the terrace above the high altar, continues up to the lantern at the top of the cathedral.

Giotto's Campanile The cathedral bell tower was begun in 1334 by Giotto, who as *capomastro* was overseer for the construction of the Duomo.

Actually he soon became more interested in the bell tower than in the church, and even made a model of the tower which is now in Siena in the Museo dell'Opera Metropolitana. Up to his death in 1337, he built the bottom part of the campanile comprised of two closed stages decorated with hexagonal and rhomboid *reliefs*, by Andrea Pisano, Luca della Robbia, Alberto Arnoldi and workshop. The relief panels on the lower band, now replaced by casts, represent the *Life of Man* with *Genesis* and *Arts* and *Industries* executed by Andrea Pisano and Luca della Robbia to Giotto's designs. His influence is clear in the relief afforded the figures and the simplified masses. The theme was influenced by the fact that Giotto had been named *capomastro* by the Corporation of the Arts, which at the time controlled the government in Florence. It was therefore in homage to his patrons that he included the following subjects in this order: the *Tilling of the Land, Sheepraising, Music, Medicine, Hunting. Weaving, Legislation, Mechanics, Navigation, Justice, Agriculture* and *Theater*. The upper row, which dates to the second half of the 14th century, represents the *Planets*, the *Virtues*, the *Liberal Arts* and the *Sacraments*. The two upper stages were carried to completion by Andrea Pisano, who took Giotto's place at the time. He created a series of sixteen niches between the pilaster strips which contained statues of the *Prophets, Sibylls* and the *Baptist*, surmounted by an equal number of false niches. Between 1350 and 1359 Francesco Talenti finished the campanile, adding two levels with the two gabled two-light windows with their lovely twisted columns and the stage with the single three-light opening. On the top, over 81 meters high, he created the large terrace supported by small arches and with an openwork balustrade. The sense for solidity is typical of Italian Gothic and the spire which Giotto had included in his original plan found no counterpart.

Museo dell'Opera del Duomo (Piazza del Duomo 9. Open: summer 9-20; winter 9-18; holid. 9-13.) Installed across from the apse of the cathedral the entrance is watched over by a fine *Bust of Cosimo I* by Giovanni Bandini. **Inside** are numerous pieces of Romanesque sculpture, statues and architectural fragments from the ancient facade of the Duomo and the Baptistery. Some of the statues to be noted on the ground floor include *Boniface VIII in the Act of Blessing, a Madonna and Child*, and the *Madonna of the Nativity* by Arnolfo di Cambio, and the famous *St. Luke* by Nanni di Banco. Nearby is a room where *illuminated manuscripts and chorales* and precious *reliquaries* are on exhibit. The museum also contains the *Magdalen*, an intense and vibrant wooden statue by Donatello.

On the first floor are the two *choir lofts*, one by Donatello and the other by Luca della Robbia, and various statues once set on Giotto's campanile. They are statues of the prophets *Habacuc, Jeremiah* and another *prophet*, all by Donatello, *Abraham* and *Isaac* by Nanni di Bartolo. In the room at the right is the fine *altar frontal of St. John the Baptist*, a large monument on which Michelozzo, Verrocchio, Antonio del Pollaiolo and Bernardo Cennini collaborated. On either side are the statues of the *Virgin Annunciate* and the *Angel Gabriel* by Jacopo della Quercia. In the room on the left are the original *relief panels* from Giotto's bell tower, made for the two tiers of decorations: they are by Andrea Pisano, Alberto Arnoldi and Luca della Robbia. Other examples of painting and sculpture include a noteworthy diptych with scenes from the *Lives of Christ and the Madonna*, of Byzantine school dating to the late 13th century, Michelangelo's *Deposition*, formerly in the Duomo (the central figure is supposed to be a self-portrait).

Museo dell'Opera del Duomo: Donatello's Choir Loft

Museo dell'Opera del Duomo: Magdalen and the Prophet Habacuc, *Donatello*

17

*Museo dell'Opera del Duomo: Pietà, Michelangelo,
and panels with the* Arts *from Giotto's Campanile*

Loggia del Bigallo This graceful Gothic structure is on the corner between
the Piazza del Duomo and the Via Calzaioli. Attributed to Alberto Arnoldi
(1352-58) it consists of two arcades richly decorated with reliefs and statues.
Once headquarters for the Compagnia della Misericordia it is now a ***Museum***
with works by important 15th- and 16th-century artists.

Museo della Loggia del Bigallo (Piazza S. Giovanni. Open: 14-19.) This is
a small but interesting museum arranged in a few rooms. Of particular note
are works by Jacopo del Sellaio, Arnolfi and Batti.

Museo dell'Opera del Duomo: relief panels from Luca della Robbia's Choir Loft

The Neptune Fountain or "Biancone" - Equestrian statue of Cosimo I de' Medici - **Loggia dei Lanzi** - **Palazzo Vecchio** - Museo Alberto Della Ragione - Church of Orsanmichele - Logge of the Mercato Nuovo and Fontana del Porcellino - Palazzo di Parte Guelfa - Museo di Storia della Scienza

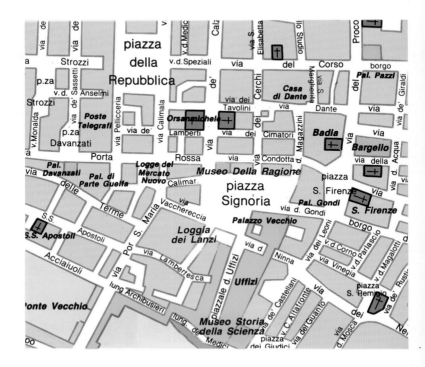

Piazza della Signoria The piazza took shape and was later enlarged between the 13th and 14th centuries thanks to the demolition of the houses of various Florentine Ghibelline families including the Uberti and the Foraboschi. The imposing complex of the *Palazzo Vecchio* towers over the piazza on the north side. To the right of the façade of the Palazzo Vecchio is the lovely *Loggia dei Lanzi*, a late Gothic structure by Simone Talenti (1376-82), enlivened by a row of important statues. To the left of the palace is the lively *Fountain of Neptune*, or Fontana di Piazza, by Bartolomeo Ammannati (1563-75) and, to one side, the *Equestrian Monument of Cosimo I* (1594) by Giambologna.

Fontana del Biancone (The Neptune Fountain) This extremely theatrical sculptural group was executed between 1563 and 1575; the powerful figure of *Neptune* looms up in the center of the Fountain, one of Ammannati's less felicitous creations (the artist may have been inspired by a drawing of Leonardo's). Much more successful are the bronze statues which represent *River Allegories* of satyrs and nymphs by Ammannati and some of his young collaborators including Giambologna.

Equestrian Statue of Cosimo I de' Medici The monument stands on the left of the Palazzo Vecchio. The work is restrained and noble with the proud pose of the *condottiero* and the imposing muscles of the horse, which Giambologna, as a mature artist, was capable of creating (1594).
The bas-reliefs of the pedestal show the *Entry of Cosimo into Siena, Pio V Giving Cosimo the Insignia of the Grand Duke, The Tuscan Senate Giving Cosimo the Title of Grand Duke*.

Palazzo Vecchio

Loggia dei Lanzi Built by Benci di Cione and Simone Talenti between 1376 and 1391, it consists of large round arches on compound piers, although there is also an emphasis on horizontal rhythms. Of late Gothic taste, the Loggia is very elegant. The fine reliefs above the piers are allegories of the *Virtues*, after designs by Agnolo Gaddi. On either side of the stairs two lions flank the access: one is an example of classic art, the other is by Flaminio Vacca (1600).

Various outstanding examples of statuary are sheltered ***inside*** the Loggia: in front, to the left, is Cellini's famous *Perseus* (1553), on the right the *Rape of the Sabines* by Giambologna (1583); at the center are *Hercules and the Centaur*, also by Giambologna (1599), *Ajax with the Body of Patrocles*, a restored piece of Hellenistic sculpture, and the *Rape of Polyxena* by Pio Fedi (1866). Six antique Roman statues of women are set against the back wall.

Loggia dei Lanzi

Loggia dei Lanzi: Hercules and the Centaur, *Giambologna;* Perseus, *Cellini*

Fountain of Neptune

Palazzo Vecchio (Quartieri Monumentali - State Apartments. Open: weekd. 9-19, holid. 8-13, closed Saturdays.) Begun in 1294 as a palace-fortress for the residence of the Priors, Arnolfo di Cambio conceived of the building as a large block crowned by crenellations.

The characteristic feature is the powerful thrust of the ***Tower*** which rises up above the palace and which echoes the terminal part.

The building is in rusticated ashlars of *pietra forte* which lend an air of austerity and atmosphere to the large three-storied building with its fine two-light windows inscribed within round arches. A row of statues is set in front of the building. On the left at the foot of the palace is the *Marzocco*, the lion which is the heraldic symbol of the city (a copy of Donatello's original of 1438, now in the Museum of the Bargello); to the right of the Marzocco is Donatello's *Judith* (1460), followed by a copy of Michelangelo's *David* and *Hercules and Cacus* (1534) by Baccio Bandinelli. On the left of the observer is the large *Fountain of Neptune*.

Immediately **inside** is the first ***Cortile*** or courtyard rebuilt by Michelozzo. The columns were stuccoed and gilded and the walls were frescoed with *Views of the Austrian Cities* by Vasari on the occasion of the wedding of Francesco de' Medici with Joan of Austria in 1565. At the center is a *fountain* by Battista del Tadda with a *winged Putto holding a spouting fish* (1467) by Andrea del Verrocchio. Under the portico is a fine sculpture of *Samson and the Philistine* by Pierino da Vinci. After the cortile two spacious flights of stairs (by Vasari) lead on each side to the ***Salone dei Cinquecento***, an enormous hall built by il Cronaca and decorated by a gost of painters chosen by

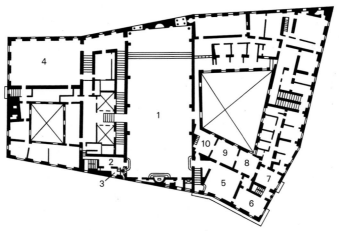

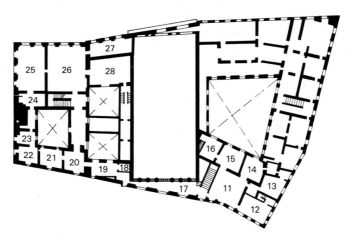

PALAZZO VECCHIO (first floor)
1) Salone dei Cinquecento
2) Studiolo of Francesco I
3) Tesoretto of Cosimo I
4) Salone dei Duecento
Quartiere of Leo X
5) Hall of Leo X
6) Hall of Clement VII
7) Hall of Giovanni dalle Bande Nere
8) Hall of Cosimo the Elder
9) Hall of Lorenzo the Magnificent
10) Hall of Cosimo I
PALAZZO VECCHIO (second floor)
Quartiere degli Elementi
11) Hall of the Elements
12) Terrace of Saturn
13) Room of Hercules

14) Room of Jupiter
15) Room of Cybele or Opis
16) Room of Ceres
17) "Ballatoio"
Quartiere of Eleonora of Toledo
18) Eleonora's Chapel
19) Green Room
20) Room of the Sabines
21) Room of Esther
22) Room of Penelope
23) Room of Gualdrada
Quartiere dei Priori
24) Chapel of the Priors
25) Audience Hall
26) Sala dei Gigli
27) Chancellery
28) Wardrobe

Vasari. The ceiling is decorated with allegorical panels of the *Triumph of the Grand Duke Cosimo I*: the four *Quarters of the City* (in the roundels in the ceiling); the sixteen *Cities of the Duchy* (in the compartments at the four corners), the six *Stories of Medici Tuscany* (in the rectangular and square compartments of the central zone), the seven *Stories of the Wars for the Conquest of Pisa* (in the rectangular, octagonal and square compartments in the left zone), and the seven *Stories of the Wars against Siena* (in the panels in the right zone).

On the entrance walls are the large allegories *of Cosimo I founding the Order of the Knights of St. Stephen*, by Passignano, and further down, the three great *Stories of the Conquest of Pisa*. These are followed by three marble sculptures: the three *Labors of Hercules* by Vincenzo De Rossi, and the statue of *Cosimo I* by Baccio Bandinelli.

The back wall has *Leo X* by Baccio Bandinelli in the central niche; in the side niches are *Giovanni delle Bande Nere* and *Alessandro de' Medici* by Ban-

Palazzo Vecchio: Salone dei Cinquecento

dinelli, a niche on the right contains *Charles V Crowned* (Bandinelli and Caccini). On the wall facing the entrance, above left, *Cosimo receiving the Insignia of the Grand Duchy from Pope Pius V*, by Cigoli; above right, *Cosimo acclaimed Duke of Florence*, also by Cigoli; further down three large *Stories of the Conquest of Siena* by Vasari.

Michelangelo's sculpture of *Victory* is on the wall to the right.

A door at the far right of the entrance leads to the **Studiolo of Francesco I**, a small chamber created by Vasari. The walls are lined with *panels* painted by Bronzino, Naldini, Santi di Tito, Stradano and with bronze *statues* by Giambologna, Ammannati, Vincenzo De Rossi. The studiolo is also decorated with stuccoes and frescoed in the lunettes with the *portraits of the Grand Duke Cosimo* and *Eleonora of Toledo*, by Bronzino.

A small staircase leads to another chamber known as **Tesoretto of Cosimo I** (by Vasari) with the Grand Duke's magnificent *desk*.

From the Salone dei Cinquecento a decorated corridor leads to the **Salone**

Palazzo Vecchio: Hercules and Diomedes, Vincenzo de' Rossi, and Studiolo of Francesco I

Palazzo Vecchio: Cappella dei Priori

dei Duecento (1441) by Giuliano and Benedetto da Maiano, with a fine carved coffered *ceiling* by Michelozzo; on the walls are *tapestries* woven in the Medici tapestry workshops on designs by Bronzino.

Entrance to the **State Apartments** is from the Salone dei Cinquecento. These include many rooms with a wealth of paintings and frescoes: the *Hall of Leo X*, frescoed in 1560 with scenes from the *Life of the Pope*; the *Hall of Clement VII*, the *Hall of Giovanni delle Bande Nere*, the *Hall of Cosimo the Elder*, the *Hall of Lorenzo the Magnificent*, the *Hall of Cosimo I*. A staircase to the second floor leads to the **Quartiere degli Elementi**, by Battista del Tasso. The name derives from the *Allegories of Earth, Air, Water and Fire* painted in the first room by Vasari.

Mention should also be made of other charming rooms: the *Room of Hercules*, the *Terrace of Saturn*, the *Terrace of Calliope*. A balcony which overlooks the Salone dei Cinquecento leads to the **Apartment of Eleonora of Toledo** by Vasari, which begins with a stupendous *Chapel* frescoed by Bronzino. Then comes the *Room of the Sabines* (once reserved for the ladies of the court), the *Room of Esther* (dining room), the *Room of Penelope*, the *Room of Gualdrada* (the bedroom of the Grand Duchess). A *Chapel* known as the «*Cappellina della Signoria*», frescoed by Ridolfo del Ghirlandaio (1514) and with a tender *Holy Family* by Mariano da Pescia on the altar, leads to the *Audience Hall*, with its fine carved *ceiling* by Giuliano da Maiano (1478). The *Sala dei Gigli*, so-named because of its decoration of golden fleur de lis on a blue field, leads to the *Sacristy* with the *Portrait of Niccoló Machiavelli*, by Santi di Tito. The bronze original of Donatello's *Judith*, restored and presented to the public in 1988, is on exhibition in the Sala dei Gigli. In the adjacent *wardrobe*, enhanced by 53 painted panels in the doors of the *Wardrobes*, is the large *Map of the World* by Danti. A staircase leads to the **Quartiere del Mezzanino**, and to the room of the old «*Ballatoio*» from whence one can go to the **Tower** of the palace where Cosimo the Elder and Savonarola were imprisoned and from which it is now possible to get a magnificent panorama of the city.

Palazzo Vecchio: Sala dei Gigli

Palazzo Vecchio: Judith, *Donatello*

Palazzo Vecchio: Putto with a fish, *Verrocchio*

Museo Alberto della Ragione (Piazza della Signoria 5. Open: 9-14, holid. 8-13, closed Tuesdays.) Installed in a small old palace in Piazza della Signoria, this rich collection of examples of contemporary Italian painting, from Rosai to De Pisis, from De Chirico to Morandi, Carra to Guttuso, and sculpture from Fontana to Manzu and Marino Marini was given to the city in 1970 by Alberto della Ragione, a well-known collector.

Church of Orsanmichele The structure was once a loggia used as a communal granary which later became an oratory. Built by Arnolfo da Cambio in 1290, it was transformed between 1337 and 1404.

The *exterior* has the aspect of a large cube with the arcades of the loggia at the base closed by a delicate late Gothic marble decoration of elegant form; the upper part is more uniform with walls in *pietra forte* and two levels of large two-light windows.

A series of tabernacles and statues runs along the walls of the building. On the Via Calzaiuoli are *St. John the Baptist* by Ghiberti (1414-16); the *Tabernacle* by Donatello and Michelozzo with the group of the *Doubting Thomas* (1464-83) by Andrea del Verrocchio, Giambologna's *St. Luke* (1601).

On the Via Orsanmichele are *St. Peter* (1408-13) by Donatello, *St. Philip* (1405-10) by Nanni di Banco, the *Quattro Santi Coronati* (four crowned martyrs) (1408) also by Nanni di Banco, the *St. George* (1416) by Donatello (bronze copy of the marble original now in the Bargello Museum).

On the Via dell'Arte della Lana are the *St. Matthew* (1420) by Ghiberti, the *St. Stephen* (1426-28) also by Ghiberti, *St. Eligius* (1415) by Nanni di Banco.

Orsanmichele: Orcagna's Tabernacle *with* Madonna *by Bernardo Daddi*

Logge del Mercato Nuovo

In the Via dei Lamberti are *St. Mark* (1411-13) by Donatello, *St. James* by a pupil of Ghiberti, *Madonna and Child* (1399) attributed to Simone Talenti, *St. John the Evangelist* by Baccio da Montelupo.

The terra-cotta *roundels* are by the Della Robbias.

Inside is a series of frescoes and panels dedicated to the *Patron Saints* (14th-16th cent.). Over the altar is a marble group of *St. Anne, Virgin and Child* by Francesco da San Gallo. But the masterpiece is the magnificent Tabernacle by Orcagna (1355-59) in International Gothic style, a structure decorated with high quality sculpture and mosaics. The *panel* framed by the tabernacle is by Bernardo Daddi.

Logge del Mercato Nuovo and Fontana del Porcellino The Loggia del Mercato Nuovo is a basic structure on a square ground plan built by G. B. del Tasso (1574-51) at the behest of Grand Duke Ferdinando I de' Medici. A characteristic market of typically Florentine craft objects (straw, leather) is held here. On the south side of the loggia is Pietro Tacca's famous *Fountain of the Boar* (1639) rebaptized *Porcellino* or Piglet by the Florentines.

Palazzo di parte Guelfa The fine 14th-century facade was restored in the 19th century while the back, which faces on the Via di Capaccio, is by Brunelleschi. The building is a mixture of various styles (14th, 15th, 16th centuries).

Inside is a large hall, by Brunelleschi, with a wooden *ceiling* by Vasari and a fine terra-cotta *lunette* by Luca della Robbia.

Museum of the History of Science (Piazza dei Giudici 1. Open: 9.30-13 Mondays, Wednesdays, Fridays also 14-17, closed Sundays). This interesting collection of objects comes from the rich collections of the Medici and the House of Lorraine. Included are some of Galileo's instruments such as a telescope and compasses, thermometers and aerometers from the Accademia del Cimento and a collection of antique surgeon's instruments.

THE BARGELLO

Palace of the Bargello - **Museo Nazionale del Bargello** - Church of Badia - Case Alighieri

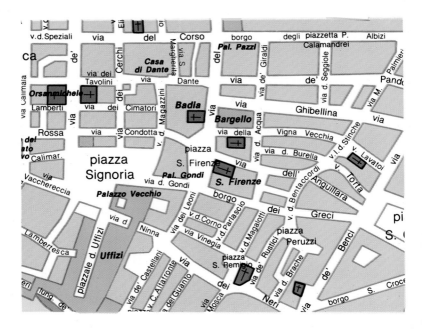

Palazzo del Bargello The Bargello palace looks like a fortress and has a powerful *crenellated tower* (the «*Volognana*») above its austere facade. It was built in 1255 as the headquarters of the Capitano del Popolo; it then became the residence of the Podestà and afterwàrds was used by the Council of Justice. From 1574 on the Bargello (or Captain of Justice) resided there and it was then called by his title. The *exterior*, divided by string courses, has architraved windows below and one or two-light windows above; the top of the building is capped by a crenellation which projects on arches and corbels.

The *interior* opens around the *courtyard* with piers supporting arcades on three sides. A picturesque *open staircase* of the 14th century by Neri di Fioravante leads to the upper *loggia*, designed by Tone di Giovanni (1319). Since 1859 the palace has been the seat of the *Museo Nazionale* which contains Renaissance sculpture and masterpieces of the minor arts from various periods.

Museo Nazionale del Bargello (Via del Proconsolo 4. Open: 9-14, holid. 9-13, closed Mondays.) The enormous *Entrance hall* on piers with solid vaulting has heraldic decorations on the walls with the coats of arms of the podestà (13th-14th cent.). There are also examples of the old Medici armory: the *Cannon of St. Paul* (1638); the so-called «*Cannon of the Falcon*» (1620), the imposing *suit of armor of Charles V* with the figures of Abundance and Neptune reproduced on the cuirass, and other interesting objects.

From here to the scenographic *Courtyard* which is irregular and unique. The coats of arms of many podestà are here and, under the portico, the picturesque insignia of the quarters and the districts into which the city was once divided. Various 16th-century *statues* set against the walls are by Bandinelli, Ammannati, Giambologna and Danti.

The courtyard leads to a *Hall* with a collection of 14th- century sculpture, including Tino da Camaino's *Madonna and Child with Angel*, a meditating *Madonna and Child* of Venetian school, the *base of a holy water stoup* by Nicola Pisano and a *Madonna between St. Peter and St. Paul* by Paolo di Giovanni (circa 1328). In the *Room* close to the open staircase are important works by Michelangelo: the *Bacchus* (1476), an early work of great power despite the softness of form, the *Pitti Tondo*, with the Madonna teaching Jesus

Bargello

and St. John to Read (1504), the *David* or Apollo (1530), the *Brutus* (1540). There are also works by Ammannati, Giambologna (including his famous Mercury -1564), Tribolo, Danti, Francavilla and Sansovino who made a *Bacchus* of his own to compete with Michelangelo's. The bronze *bust of Cosimo I* by Cellini, made for Portoferraio in Elba and brought back in 1781, is also in the same room.

The **open Staircase** leads to the **Loggia**, ornamented with works by various 16th- century artists.

The first room to the right, once the Salone del Consiglio Generale, is now the **Donatello Room** and contains many of his works such as the *St. George* (1416) with its self-contained energy, made for the niche in Orsanmichele; the young *St. John*, slender and mystical; the marble *David* (1408); and the bronze *David*, the first delicate Renaissance nude made around 1430. Also by Donatello are the *Marzocco*, the symbol of the city, and the lively bronze *Amor-Attis*, revealing a classic influence. In addition to works by Luca della Robbia, Ghiberti, Vecchietta and Agostino di Duccio, the room also contains the *trial panels* which Ghiberti and Brunelleschi made in 1402 for the competition (there were six contestants) for the second doors of the Florentine Baptistery. Ghiberti's relief succeeds in giving us an organically complete vision of the story of the *Sacrifice of Isaac* while Brunelleschi's panel, well articulated as it is, gives the impression of a juxtaposition of parts.

Access to the **Collection of Decorative Arts**, mostly based on the donation of the Carrand Collections, is from the hall.

Goldwork and *enamels* from the Middle Ages to the 16th century, *seals* and various metal objects are in the **Salone del Podestà**.

In the adjacent **Cappella del Podestà**, where those condemned to death passed their last hours, there are Giottesque frescoes with *Paradise*, *Hell* and

31

Bargello: Hall of Renaissance sculpture

Bargello: Brutus *and* Bacchus,
Michelangelo

Bargello: upper loggia

Stories of the Saints. The floor is completed by the **Sala degli Avori**, with rare carvings from antiquity to the 15th century; the **Sala delle Oreficerie**, with numerous works of sacred art, and the **Sala delle Majoliche**.

The second floor of the Bargello contains other rooms dedicated to great artists: the first, known as the **Giovanni della Robbia Room**, contains a number of the master's sculptures including the predella with *Christ and Saints*, *St. Dominic*, the *Pietà* and the *Annunciation*.

The following **Andrea della Robbia room** houses the *Madonna degli Architetti* and other works in glazed terracotta. In the **Verrocchio Room** are the *Resurrection*, the *bust of a young woman*, the *Madonna and Child*, the bronze *David* and other works by the master as well as various *busts* and sculpture by Mino da Fiesole and the group of *Hercules and Antaeus* by Pollaiolo, with the vibrating force of the two struggling figures. Other bronze sculpture is in the **Sala dei Bronzetti** with the *mantelpiece of Casa Borgherini* by Benedetto da Rovezzano; the **Sala delle Armi** houses military paraphernalia from the Middle Ages to the 17th century.

The museum is completed by the **Sala della Torre** with tapestries and the **Medagliere Mediceo** with works by artists such as Pisanello, Cellini, Michelozzo and others.

The Badia The church of Badia in Cistercian style was founded before the 11th century but was completely reconstructed in the 17th century.

The **facade** has a fine portal by Benedetto da Rovezzano (1495).

The lovely slender **campanile** still has some of its Romanesque structure at the base (1310) but the top is Gothic. The **interior** is a Greek cross plan and contains a series of masterpieces of Renaissance sculpture: to the right of the entrance is the *tomb of Giannotto Pandolfini*, by Rossellino's workshop; the fine bas-relief of the *Madonna and Child with SS. Leonardo and Lorenzo* (1464-69) is by Mino da Fiesole to whom the *tomb of Bernardo Giugni* (1469-81) is also attributed.

The left chapel leads to a room of the original construction frescoed by a follower of Giotto, probably Buffalmacco (1314); on the wall to the left of the entrance the fine panel of the *Apparition of the Virgin to St. Bernard* (1480), is one of Filippino Lippi's finest works.

Near the apse is the entrance to the **Chiostro degli Aranci** with a fourteenth-century fresco cycle of *Scenes from the life of St. Bernard* by an unknown painter.

Case Alighieri The complex of the Alighieri houses, mostly restored, lies in a widening of the lanes and alleys of the city center. At present the small piazza, squeezed between two tower-houses, has a low building on one side, with a long shed roof on brackets that covers the entrance; inside: exhibitions and the well.

UFFIZI GALLERY

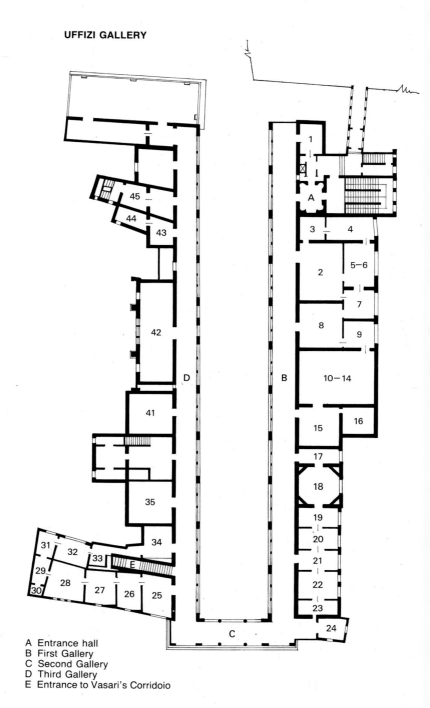

A Entrance hall
B First Gallery
C Second Gallery
D Third Gallery
E Entrance to Vasari's Corridoio

Uffizi (Loggiato degli Uffizi 6. Open: weekd. 9-14, holid. 9-13, closed Mondays.) The gallery of the Uffizi is the most famous picture gallery in Italy and one of the best known in the world. It furnishes a complete panorama of the various schools of Florentine painting, represented by important works and authentic masterpieces. It also includes numerous collections of other Italian schools (particularly the Venetian) and a fine group of Flemish paintings, as well as the famous collection of self-portraits. To be noted also are the antique statues and an extensive collection of tapestries.

The Uffizi was commissioned from Giorgio Vasari by the Medicis as administrative and judicial offices (thence the name). Begun in 1560 and finished twenty years later, the two wings with a loggiato at the bottom are connected by a third wing with arches along the Arno. On either side of the central courtyard powerful piers contain niches with 19th-century statues of illustrious Tuscans, while the upper floors of the building have windows (1st floor) and a running loggia (2nd floor).

In addition to the Gallery, which is on the second floor, the building houses the **State Archives** which contain rare documents from the city's history. On the ground floor note should be taken of the remains of the Romanesque church of **San Piero Scheraggio** (brought to light and restored in 1971) with fine frescoes by Andrea del Castagno. On the first floor is the **Gabinetto dei Disegni e delle Stampe** (Drawing and Print Cabinet), an imposing collection begun in the 17th century at the behest of Cardinal Leopoldo de' Medici. The visit to the Gallery begins on the second floor. This great museum did not become public patrimony until 1737, a gift of Anna Maria Ludovica de' Medici, the last of this prestigious family. The gallery consists of 45 rooms divided into sections.

Uffizi: courtyard

Uffizi: upper gallery

Room 1 (The Archaeological Room). The room contains a *torso* in green basalt, Roman copy of a Doryphoros by Polykleitos.

Room 2 (Tuscan painting of the 13th century and Giotto). This room contains some of the greatest works of this period such as the *Santa Trinita Madonna* by Cimabue (1285), a fundamental work which testifies to the passage from the Byzantine and Romanesque tradition to a major awareness of the development of forms. The figures are rigorously symmetrical in relation to the fine architecture of the throne. The room also contains the *Rucellai Madonna (Madonna Enthroned with Six Angels)* (1285) by the Sienese painter Duccio da Boninsegna, a work laid out along the lines of Cimabue's pictorial rhythms but which is original in its composition, grace and softness of forms; and Giotto's *Ognissanti Madonna (Madonna and Child Enthroned with Angels and Saints)* (1310) which marks the beginning of a new direction in Italian figural art. To be noted are the layout of the picture based on the superposition and moving back into space of the figures which already hint at the beginnings of perspective.

Room 3 (Sienese painting of the 14th century). On exhibition are works by Pietro and Ambrogio Lorenzetti, as well as the splendid *Annunciation with Saints* (1333) by Simone Martini, a large triptych focussed on the intimate and touching dialogue between Gabriel and the Virgin; the figures at the sides of *Saints Ansano and Giulitta* are by Lippo Memmi, Simone Martini's brother-in-law.

Room 4 (Florentine painting of the 14th century). Many works by the most prestigious Florentine masters are collected here: Taddeo Gaddi, Bernardo Daddi, Giottino, Giovanni da Milano.

Room 5-6 (International Gothic). Particularly striking in this room are the brilliantly colored *Adoration of the Magi* (1425) by Gentile da Fabriano, a panel populated by a host of figures in rich costumes, and Lorenzo Monaco's exuberant triptych of the *Coronation of the Virgin* (1413).

Room 7 (Early Renaissance Florentine painting). The outstanding paintings in this room include the *Madonna and Child with St. Anne* (1420-24) by Masaccio and terminated by Masolino da Panicale (the sculptural group of the Virgin and Child, touching in its realism, is by Masaccio); the *Battle of San Romano* (1456) by Paolo Uccello, a large work in three panels of which only one, crowded with knights in battle, is in the Uffizi.

Here in his daring search for perspective the artist has created a fascinating almost abstract ensemble. Then there are the *Portraits of Federico da Mon-*

Uffizi: Ognissanti Madonna, *Giotto;* Santa Trinita Madonna, *Cimabue*

Uffizi: Annunciation, *Simone Martini*

37

Uffizi: Portraits of the Dukes of Urbino, *Piero della Francesca*

tefeltro *and his wife* Batista Sforza (1465), two splendid profiles by Piero della Francesca, who has achieved a remarkable purity of line and a profound introspection.

Room 8 (Florentine painting of the 15th century). Also known as the Filippo Lippi room because so many of the works of this great master are on exhibit here, including the *Adoration of the Child with Saints*, the *Coronation of the Virgin*, the *Madonna and Child with an Angel*, as well as interesting works

Uffizi: Madonna of the Magnificat, *Botticelli*

Uffizi: Birth of Venus, *Botticelli*

by Alessio Baldovinetti, such as the *Madonna and Child with Saints* and the *Annunciation*. In addition the room contains early works by Botticelli such as the *Madonna of the Rose Garden*, and the *Madonna Enthroned and Saints* by Lorenzo di Pietro called Vecchietta.

Room 9 (Florentine painting of the 15th century, known also as the Pollaiolo room). This room contains numerous works by the brothers Antonio and Piero del Pollaiolo. By Antonio let us recall the famous *Portrait of a Lady, Hercules and Antaeus*; and by Piero, *Temperance* and the *Portrait of Galeazzo Maria Sforza*.

Room 10-14 (The Botticelli rooms). Some of the greatest masterpieces of the artist and of the entire 15th century are hung here, including the famous *Primavera* (1477-78), a magnificent allegory in an atmosphere of classicizing taste. The soft airy figures and the extreme wealth of details have made the painting one of the most famous pictures in art history. Just as celebrated is the *Birth of Venus* where the softly modeled figure of the goddess standing on a shell, or rather floating in air with incredible lightness, dominates the picture. Botticelli also painted the realistic *Adoration of the Magi*, the touch-

Uffizi: Primavera, *Botticelli*

Uffizi: Annunciation, *Leonardo da Vinci*

Uffizi: Virgin and Child with Saints, *Ghirlandaio*

ing *Annunciation* and the sophisticated *Madonna of the Magnificat* and the *Madonna of the Pomegranate*. Mention should also be made of the festive colorful *Adoration of the Magi* by Filippino Lippi and panel paintings by Lorenzo di Credi and Ghirlandaio.

Room 15 (Dedicated to artists active between the 15th and 16th centuries, known also as the Leonardo room). Among the works on exhibit let us recall Verrocchio's *Baptism of Christ* where Leonardo's unmistakable touch can be seen in the face of the angel in profile and the landscape in the background; Leonardo's *Adoration of the Magi* which, even though unfinished, is considered the great artist first masterpiece, and his *Annunciation*, a work that is still 15th-century in its layout but already bears the unmistakable mark of his hand.

Room 16 (Room of the Maps). Works exhibited here include important paintings by Hans Memling, such as the *Madonna and Child Enthroned with two Angels, Saint Benedict*, the stupendous *Portrait of a Man* and *Portrait of Benedetto Portinari*.

Room 17 (Room of the Hermaphrodite). This small room contains the sculpture of the *Hermaphrodite* and the group of *Cupid and Psyche*.

Room 18 (Known also as the Tribune). Its name was determined by the magnificent *tribune* by Buontalenti (1585-89), octagonal in plan, with fine decorations in the cupola where the sections have mother-of-pearl applications. In addition to examples of antique sculpture, the room contains a vast collection of 16th- century portraits including Andrea del Sarto's enigmatic *Portrait of a Lady* and outstanding portraits by Bronzino, Pontormo, Rosso Fiorentino and many other Mannerist artists. The center of the room is dominated by the *Medici Venus*, a first-century B.C. copy of a Greek original of the 5th century B.C.. It is one of the most famous examples of classical sculpture in Florence - a marble with softly modelled forms and luminous effects of light and dark.

Room 19 (The Signorelli and Perugino Room). Noteworthy is the *Holy Family*, a tondo by Luca Signorelli with an intimate supernatural atmosphere; the famous *Madonna and Child* also by Signorelli, and some intense portraits by Perugino, including those of *Don Biagio Milanesi* and *Baldassare Vallombrosano*, and that of *Francesco delle Opere*, paintings of a particularly introspective nature.

Room 20 (Dürer and German Painting). The room contains exemplary portraits by Lukas Cranach the Elder including the famous *Portrait of Luther* and of his wife *Caterina Bore*, that of *Friedrich III* and *Johann I, Elector of Saxony*. But the most important artist represented is Albrecht Dürer with his *Adoration of the Magi*, a painting of great sweep and monumentality, the *Apostle Philip*, the *Large Calvary* and the deeply moving *Portrait of his Father*.

Room 21 (The Bellini and Giorgione Room including Venetian 15th- century painting). Outstanding are Giovanni Bellini's imaginative *Sacred Allegory*, with its fascinating contemplative air, illuminated by beams of mystical light, and Giorgione's two masterpieces, *Moses undergoes Trial by Fire* and the *Judgement of Solomon*.

Room 22 (Flemish and German Masters). To be noted are the *Adoration of the Magi* by Gerard David and the *Portrait of Sir Richard Southwell* by Hans Holbein.

Room 23 (The Correggio Room). Particularly striking are the *Madonna and Child in Glory*, the popular and tender *Rest on the Flight into Egypt*, and the moving *Adoration of the Child*, all by the founder of the Emilian school, Antonio Allegri called Correggio. Also of interest are two rather naive portraits attributed to Raphael's early years, the portrait of *Elisabetta Gonzaga* and that of *Guidobaldo da Montefeltro*.

Room 24 (The Room of Miniatures). This room contains a number of Italian, French, German and English miniatures dating from the 15th to the 18th centuries.

Room 25 (The Michelangelo Room). In addition to important paintings such as Mariotto Albertinelli's *Visitation*, his *Annunciation* and *Nativity*, and Rosso Fiorentino's *Moses Defends the Daughters of Jethro*, attention centers on the *Holy Family* or *Doni Tondo* by Michelangelo, the artist's only finished panel

Uffizi: Adoration of the Kings, *Gentile da Fabriano*

Uffizi: Holy Family, *or* Doni Tondo, *Michelangelo*

painting. The group of three holy figures looms up in the small space and the monumentality and sculptural quality that were to characterize the artist are already evident here.

Room 26 (The Raphael and Andrea del Sarto Room). The room contains a wealth of masterpieces including Andrea del Sarto's *St James* and his statuesque *Madonna of the Harpies* and, above all, Raphael's *Pope Leo X with Cardinals Giulio de' Medici and Luigi de' Rossi*, one of the artist's finest works which reveals his capacities for psychological introspection, evident in the search for expression in the features of the three figures, and a marvelous attention to detail. Raphael's transparent *Madonna of the Goldfinch* is also particularly lovely. It is an early work but it has already left Perugino's composition behind and is clearly influenced in its pyramidal composition by Leonardo.

Room 27 (The Pontormo and Rosso Fiorentino Room) The room is almost entirely dedicated to the great Florentine Mannerist painters. Note particularly Pontormo's haunting *Supper at Emmaus* and Rosso Fiorentino's intimate *Madonna and Child.*

Room 28 (The Titian Room) The room contains a wealth of masterpieces by the great Venetian painter: the penetrating *Portrait of Bishop Ludovico Beccadilli*, the famous *Venus and Cupid* and the *Portraits of Eleonora Gonzaga della Rovere and Francesco Maria della Rovere.* But the finest of all is the *Venus of Urbino*, one of the greatest works of Titian's maturity: a magnificent nude in warm tones and frank sensuality.

Room 29 (The Parmigianino Room). In addition to various important works by painters such as Luca Cambiaso, Girolamo da Carpi, Beccafumi and Perin del Vaga, the room contains various masterpieces by Parmigianino such as the *Portrait of a Man, Madonna and Child with Saints* and the elegant

43

Uffizi: Slaughter of the Innocents, *Daniele da Volterra*

sophisticated *Madonna of the Long Neck*.

Room 30 (Emilian Painting). This room houses works by Emilian artists of the 16th century, such as Niccolò Pisano, Niccolò dell'Abate, Dosso Dossi.

Room 31 (Room of Dosso Dossi). In addition to the *Sorcery* by Dossi, the room contains various works by Sebastiano del Piombo and Lorenzo Lotto.

Room 32 (Room of Sebastiano del Piombo). In addition to a fine *Sacra Conversazione* by Lorenzo Lotto and the *Portrait of a Knight* and the *Portrait of a Man* by Paris Bordone, note should be taken of Sebastiano del Piombo's famous *Death of Adonis*, influenced by Raphael in the softness of color and by Michelangelo in the powerful forms.

Room 33 (16th-century Painting and Foreign Artists). In particular mention should be made of the powerful portrait of *François I of France on Horseback* by François Clouet; *Christ Carrying the Cross* by Luis de Morales, a painting imbued with realism and human suffering; as well as a goodly number of paintings by Florentine artists of the late 16th century.

Room 34 (The Veronese Room). Particularly striking are the *Holy Family with Saint Barbara* (in restoration), with its warmth and intense vibrant colors, the small *Saint Agatha Crowned by Angels*, and above all the *Annunciation*, a painting with an original composition with its illusionistic perspective architecture, all by Veronese. Mention should also be made of Moroni's famous *Portrait of a Man with a Book* and the mystical *Transfiguration* by Savoldo.

Room 35 (The Tintoretto and Barocci Room). This room contains some of the masterpieces by late Mannerist painters: a penetrating *Portrait of a Man* by Tintoretto, his *Portrait of Jacopo Sansovino* and his soft *Leda and the Swan*, a canvas with intense colors and an almost hallucinatory luminosity. Together are to be found various paintings by Federico Barocci, the greatest Mannerist painter of central Italy, represented by his large canvas of the *Madonna del Popolo*, his most famous painting, a lively surprising image, full of figures who point to the figure of the Virgin in astonishment, his *Noli Me Tangere*, a delicate painting, and then his *Portrait of a Girl* and the *Stigmata of St. Francis*, so simple and immediate in its composition.

Room 41 (The Rubens Room) Imposing canvases of *Henry IV at the Battle*

44

Uffizi: Marie Henriette of France, *Jean-Marc Nattier*

of Ivry and the *Triumphal Entrance of Henry IV into Paris*, two of the most valid works of Rubens' maturity, are hung here. Mention should also be made of a fine series of *Portraits* by Van Dyck, Sustermans and Rubens.

Room 42 (The Niobe Room). The room was commissioned from Gaspare Maria Paoletti in 1779 by the grand duke Pietro Leopoldo. The statues of the group of the *Niobids* discovered in Rome in 1583 and transferred to Florence in 1775 are on exhibition here. The statues are Roman copies of Hellenistic originals of the 3rd and 2nd centuries B.C.

Room 43 (The Caravaggio Room). Three basic works by Caravaggio at once strike the eye: the *Medusa*, an impressive image intensified by the violent beams of light which fall on her features; the *Adolescent Bacchus*, an early work representing a youth, almost an ephebus, and the dramatic *Sacrifice of Isaac* where, in true Caravaggesque style, a beam of light illuminates the face of the boy who is about to be sacrificed.

Room 44 (The Rembrandt Room). The room contains various masterpieces by Rembrandt: the two lovely *Self-Portraits* - the study of himself as an old man characterized by his personal capacity for introspection, and that of the artist as a young man with its self-assured almost arrogant expression. Note also Rembrandt's famous *Portrait of an Old Man*, also called *The Rabbi*, which reveals the artist's acute eye and gift for psychological analysis.

Room 45 (Painting of the 18th Century). This is the last room in the Gallery. A number of 18th-century works, particularly by Italian and French painters, are on exhibit here. There are canvases by great *vedutisti* (panorama painters) such as Canaletto, Bellotto and Francesco Guardi, and expert artists from north of the Alps such as Jean Baptiste Simeon Chardin and Jean Etienne Liotard as well as a series of portraits by Rosalba Carriera. Between the door leading to Room 25 and the one leading to Room 34 is the entrance staircase to **Vasari's Corridor**, built by Vasari in 1565 and joining the Gallery to Palazzo Pitti. Along the Corridor are hung important paintings by Italian and non-Italian artists and the entire painting collection of *Self-Portraits* (Raphael, Titian, Bernini, Rubens, Rembrandt, Velazquez, Canova, David, Ingres, Corot, Delacroix, and many others) up to the artists of the 20th century.

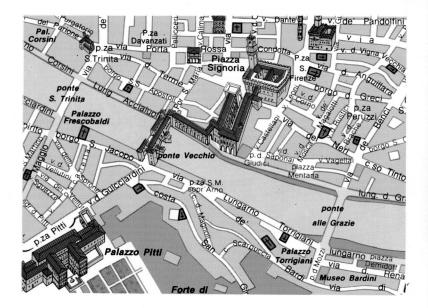

Ponte Vecchio The oldest bridge in the city, it was built as it is now in 1345 by Neri di Fioravante, with its elegant three-arched span.

A characteristic feature of the bridge is the rows of small houses on either side; in the 14th century their aspect was much more regular, and they were transformed as time passed until they became picturesquely varied as they are now. At about the center of the span over the river, the buildings are interrupted and an opening furnishes a fine view of the Arno and the other bridges. A bronze bust of *Benvenuto Cellini* by Raffaello Romanelli (1900) has been placed here.

Above the houses, on the upstream side of the bridge, is *Vasari's Corridor*, built by Vasari so Cosimo could go from Palazzo Pitti to Palazzo Vecchio. The shops on either side of the bridge are still in use and are workshops for artisan goldsmiths.

Church of San Felice The church of San Felice has a Renaissance **Facade** by Michelozzo. Of note are the carved wooden 15th-century *doors*. The building dates to the Middle Ages but it was frequently remodeled between the 14th and 16th centuries.

The **interior** is small with three aisles on columns and a large 16th-century gallery over the first half. Noteworthy on the first altar to the right is the fresco with the *Pietà* by Nicola Gerini; a *Madonna and Saints* by Rodolfo del Ghirlandaio and a fresco in the lunette with the *Assumption* by an unknown 14th-century painter at the sixth altar. Seventh altar, left, the fresco with *St. Felix resuscitating St. Maximus of Nola* (1635) by Giovanni da San Giovanni (the *Angels* are by Volterrano). Above on the wall of the Nuns' Gallery is a painted *Cross* in the style of Giotto, while the triptych on the first altar to the left with *SS. Rocco, Anthony Abbot and Catherine of Siena* (1480) is attributed to Filippino Lippi or a follower of Botticelli.

Museo Bardini (Piazza de' Mozzi 1. Open: 9-14, holid. 8-13, closed Wednesdays.) This collection contains a wealth of important paintings, period furniture, precious tapestries, archaeological objects from Roman times, weapons and wooden sculpture. Outstanding are a bust of *St. John* by Andrea Sansovino; a marble *Charity* by Tino di Camaino; some *terracottas* by the Della Robbia; a panel with *St. Michael Archangel* by Antonio del Pollaiolo.

Ponte Vecchio

Ponte Vecchio and Bust of Benvenuto Cellini, *Raffaello Romanelli*

Galleria Corsini - Church of Santa Trinita - Column of Justice - Church of SS. Apostoli - Palazzo Davanzati - Museo della Casa Antica Fiorentina - Palazzo Strozzi - Church of Santa Maria Maggiore - Palazzo Rucellai - Rucellai Loggia - Rucellai Chapel

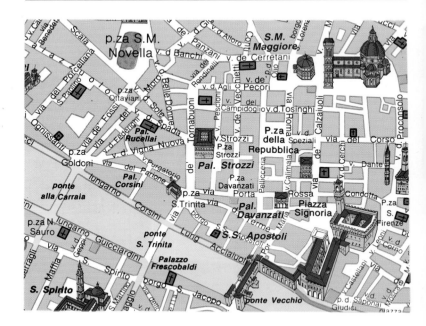

Ponte Santa Trinita After Ponte Vecchio, this is considered the most beautiful bridge in the city. It was built by Bartolomeo Ammannati, with Michelangelo advising on the design. Fine statues are set at the entrances to the bridge: on the side towards the city *Primavera* (Spring) by Pietro Francavilla is on the left, and *Estate* (Summer) by Cacini is one the right. On the opposite side are *Autumn*, also by Cacini, and *Inverno* (Winter) by Taddeo Landini.

Galleria Corsini Installed in Palazzo Corsini, the Gallery includes a rich selection of paintings of the 16th and 17th centuries, by great artists such as Signorelli, Filippino Lippi, Raphael, Andrea del Sarto and Pontormo.

Church of Santa Trìnita The church already existed in the 11th century and was rebuilt and enlarged in the 13th and 14th centuries.
The **facade** is linear and decorated with a lovely stone *facing* by Buontalenti (1593).
The **interior** is simple and severe, with three aisles separated by piers. In the first chapel of the right aisle the eye lights on a fine 14th-century *Crucifix*; in the third, a *Madonna Enthroned with Saints* by Neri di Bicci (1491); in the fourth the *Annunciation* by Lorenzo Monaco (1425) and in the fifth, a lovely *altar* by Benedetto da Maiano.
After the end of the crossing comes the **Sacristy** and then the **Sassetti Chapel**. The fresco over the entrance arch depicts the *Tiburtine Sibyl announcing the Birth of Christ to Augustus*; inside, *Scenes from the Life of St. Francis*; behind the altar, the *Miracle of the Resuscitated Child*; above the altar, *St. Francis Receiving the Rule from Pope Honorius*, all by Ghirlandaio (1483-86). On the walls are the *tombs of the Sassetti family*, by Giuliano da Sangallo and, on the altar, the *Adoration of the Shepherds*, also by Ghirlandaio.
Next comes the **Cappella Maggiore** or Chancel with a triptych of the *Trinity*

Ponte Santa Trinita

and Saints by Mariotti di Nardo (1416) on a 15th-century altar while remains of *frescoes* by Alessio Baldovinetti are in the vault. In the second chapel is the *tomb of the bishop of Fiesole Benozzo Federici*, a stupendous work by Luca della Robbia, decorated with a charming frieze of painted and glazed terra-cotta tiles. In the fifth chapel of the left aisle is a wooden statue of the *Magdalen* begun by Desiderio da Settignano (1464) and finished by Benedetto da Maiano (1468). Mention should be made, in the third chapel, of an *Annunciation* by Neri di Bicci (1491) and in the fouth chapel of a *Coronation of the Virgin*, probably by a pupil of Neri (1491).

Ponte Santa Trinita: Spring, *Pietro Francavilla, and* Summer, *Giovanni Caccini*

Church of Santa Trinita: Adoration of the Shepherds, *Ghirlandaio*

49

Column of Justice This tall column in oriental granite came from the baths of Caracalla in Rome; in 1560 it was presented by Pius IV to Cosimo I, who had it set in the piazza in memory of the victory of Montemurlo (1537). On top is a porphyry state of a female figure with a bronze cloak, allegory of Justice, a work by Tadda (1581).

Church of the SS. Apostoli Begun in 1075, the church of the SS. Apostoli was a prototype for many other Florentine churches with its archaic Roman forms. Even though it is of modest size, the building has considerable solemnity.
The *interior* is full of atmosphere with a fine painted timber shed roof on compound piers which articulate the church into three aisles.
On the third altar of the *right aisle* is a panel with the *Immaculate Conception* by Giorgio Vasari (one of his best works). The apse contains the *tomb of the archbishop Antonio Altoviti* executed on designs by G. B. Dosio (1574). To be noted in the *left aisle* is a *tabernacle* by Andrea della Robbia, the *tomb of Donato Acciaioli* (1339) of Pisan school, and the *tomb of Oddo Altoviti* by Bernardo da Rovezzano (1507).

Palazzo Davanzati Built around 1330, the lower story is of rusticated *pietra forte*; in the upper floors the external facing is smoother and broken by rhythmic series of windows with the typical Florentine arch with its round arched intrados. Above is the 15th-century *terrace* covered by a gabled watershed. The palace is one of the most distinguished examples of private 14th-century dwelling houses and is today occupied by the *Museo della Casa Fiorentina*, an interesting collection of furniture and interior furnishings of the 15th and 16th centuries.

Museo della Casa Antica Fiorentina (Via Porta Rossa 13. Open: 9-14, holid. 9-13, closed Mondays.) The museum contains perfect reconstructions of period rooms, particularly of the 15th and 16th centuries. Dining rooms, wedding chambers, meeting halls are all furnished with magnificent tapestries, small-scale sculpture and various household objects. The *staircase* of the striking *internal courtyard* leads to the exhibition rooms. To be noted is the presence on various walls of old notices (dating from the time when the building was used as public offices) which have today been collected into an amusing *corpus* which gives us an insight into the Florence that once was.

Palazzo Strozzi This typical example of a Renaissance palace was designed by Benedetto da Maiano in 1489. Construction work continued, under various overseers, until 1538 when the building was brought to a halt, incomplete as it was on the south side.
The lower story in rusticated *pietra forte* ashlar is by Benedetto and is characterized by the wide *portal* with the arches in rusticated ashlar and the row of rectangular windows; the upper zone is attributed to il Cronaca, as are the two dentellated cornice moldings which jut out over the floors, of a classicizing style, and the cornice at the top of the building. On the front, as in the sides, the upper floors are pierced by rows of two-light windows with the external arch in rusticated ashlars.
The *interior* of the palace faces on a *courtyard* in several floors, supported below by columns, in the intermediate floor by engaged pilasters and at the top by columns which form a fine loggia.
The many rooms, some of which still maintain their Renaissance aspect, are currently used as space for cultural manifestations and art exhibitions.

Church of Santa Maria Maggiore Begun in the 10th century in Romanesque style, S. Maria Maggiore was almost completely rebuilt in Gothic style at the end of the 13th century.
The linear severe *facade* has a lovely 14th-century *Madonna* of Pisan school on the pointed arch portal. The *interior*, in Cistercian style, is extremely simple with three aisles with pointed arches on square piers with dentilled cornices and square chapels. Traces of 14th-century frescoes by Agnolo Daddi, Spinello Aretino, Paolo Uccello and Masaccio are still to be found on some of the piers.
The two episodes from the *Story of King Herod*, painted in the style of Spinello Aretino in the *Cappella Maggiore*, are particularly fine. In the left chapel is a relief in gilded wood of a *Madonna and Child*, while in the right aisle

Palazzo Davanzati

Palazzo Strozzi

is a noteworthy altar on which is a painting of *Saint Rita* by the contemporary artist Primo Conti.

Palazzo Rucellai The design for the palace was created for the Rucellai by Leon Battista Alberti, and the project was carried out by Rossellino between 1446 and 1451.
The classicizing **facade** is articulated into three stories by horizontal string-courses with decorations supported by pilasters. These divide the flattened rustication into zones, with simple windows set into the lower story and divided windows into the upper stories.

The Rucellai Loggia Opposite the palace the Rucellai family had the *loggia* built in a widening at the fork of the street. The three arches on piers were built between 1460 and 1466 and the 17th-century walls which closed the openings have now been removed.

Rucellai Chapel Not far from their palace the Rucellai had their *chapel* where they commissioned the **Shrine of the Holy Sepulcher** from Alberti. The rectangular apsed structure has Corinthian pilasters and a crenellated entablature along the top of the black and white marble walls. The whole is covered by a baldachin with a dome. Inside are *frescoes* by Baldovinetti and a terra-cotta *Christ*.

Palazzo Rucellai

Church of Santa Maria Maggiore

Church of Santa Maria Novella - Obelisks of Piazza Santa Maria Novella - Loggia of San Paolo - Church of Ognissanti - Cenacolo di Foligno

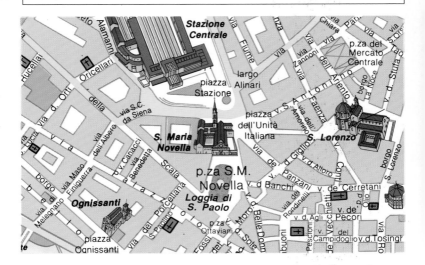

Church of Santa Maria Novella Begun in 1279 by Sisto da Firenze and Ristoro da Campi, it was finished in 1348 by Jacopo Talenti with the campanile in Gothic style (1330).

The marvelous **facade** was finished between 1456 and 1470 by Leon Battista Alberti, who designed the portal and the part above is divided into compartments by inlaid marble and framed by the coats of arms (sails of Fortune) of the Rucellai who commissioned the great work.

Two large volutes, turned upside down, join the masses at the sides with the center, divided by four engaged pilasters and terminated by a triangular pediment.

The **interior** is subdivided into a nave and two aisles by piers carrying pointed vaults. A fine mosaic *Nativity* based on a cartoon by Filippo Lippi is set over the central door.

In the second bay of the **right aisle** is the *tomb of the Beata Villana*, by Rossellino (1451), and the **Cappella della Pura**, a Renaissance structure built in honor of a miracle-working *Madonna*, a 14th-century fresco, in the left-hand corner.

In the right arm of the crossing is the terra-cotta *bust of St. Antonine* and, above, the *tomb of Tedice Aliotti, Bishop of Fiesole,* by Tino di Camaino. A flight of steps leads to the **Rucellai Chapel** with remains of frescoes of the *Martyrdom of St. Catherine* by Giuliano Bugiardini; at the center of the pavement is the fine *tombslab for Leonardo Dati* by Ghiberti. From the crossing there is access to the **Bardi Chapel** with the *Madonna of the Rosary* by Vasari (1568) and remains of 14th-century *frescoes*; the **Chapel of Filippo Strozzi the Elder** with important frescoes, including scenes from the *Lives of St. Philip and St. John Evangelist* by Filippino Lippi (1503). On the back wall is the *tomb of Filippo Strozzi* by Benedetto da Maiano (1491); the **Chancel (or Cappella Maggiore)** of the Tornabuoni, with a fine bronze *Crucifix* by Giambologna on the altar and frescoes on the vault and on the walls with scenes from the *Lives of St. John the Baptist* (on the right) and *of the Virgin* (on the left) by Domenico Ghirlandaio (late 15th century).

The *Gondi Chapel*, decorated by Giuliano da Sangallo, has fragments of *frescoes* by 13th-century Greek painters and on the back wall the famous *Crucifix* by Brunelleschi; next come the **Gaddi Chapel** whith the *Miracle of Jesus* by Bronzino on the altar; the **Chapel of the Strozzi family of Mantua** with frescoes of the *Last Judgement* on the back wall, with *Hell* on the right and *Paradise* on the left, by Nardo di Cione or by Orcagna. A large panel of the *Triumphant Christ* by Orcagna (1357) is on the altar.

Then comes the **Sacristy**, built by Jacopo Talenti (1350); on the left, a marble

Church of Santa Maria Novella

lavabo in a glazed terra-cotta niche by Giovanni della Robbia (1498).
Masaccio's *Trinity*, an extremely important fresco, is in the **left aisle**; on the
second pier is a *pulpit* designed by Brunelleschi, with classical decorative elements and bas-reliefs by Buggiano (1462). The gate to the left of the facade
leads to the Cloisters of the **Large Convent** (now used for civilian and military purposes): the **First Cloister** (or «Chiostro Verde») is the oldest, in
Romanesque style. Various frescoes with *scenes from the Old Testament* by
Paolo Uccello have been detached and are now exhibited in the refectory.
Nearby is the famous **Spanish Chapel** built by Jacopo Talenti (1359) in
honor of St. Thomas of Aquinas: on the entrance wall are the scenes from
the *Life of St. Peter Martyr* and above, in the vault, the *Ascension*. The side
walls are decorated with allegories of the *Triumph of Wisdom and the Church
Militant and Triumphant* by Andrea di Buonaiuto (1366-68).
The so-called **Chiostrino dei Morti** (Cloister of the Dead) in Romanesque
style, which contains a number of *tomb slabs*, leads to the **Chiostro Grande**,
the largest in the city with over fifty arches and completely frescoed by the

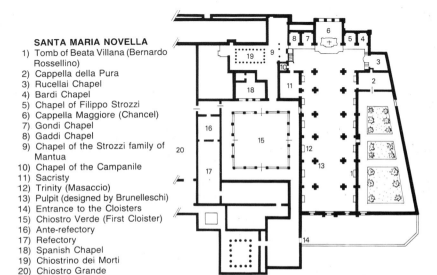

SANTA MARIA NOVELLA
1) Tomb of Beata Villana (Bernardo Rossellino)
2) Cappella della Pura
3) Rucellai Chapel
4) Bardi Chapel
5) Chapel of Filippo Strozzi
6) Cappella Maggiore (Chancel)
7) Gondi Chapel
8) Gaddi Chapel
9) Chapel of the Strozzi family of Mantua
10) Chapel of the Campanile
11) Sacristy
12) Trinity (Masaccio)
13) Pulpit (designed by Brunelleschi)
14) Entrance to the Cloisters
15) Chiostro Verde (First Cloister)
16) Ante-refectory
17) Refectory
18) Spanish Chapel
19) Chiostrino dei Morti
20) Chiostro Grande

53

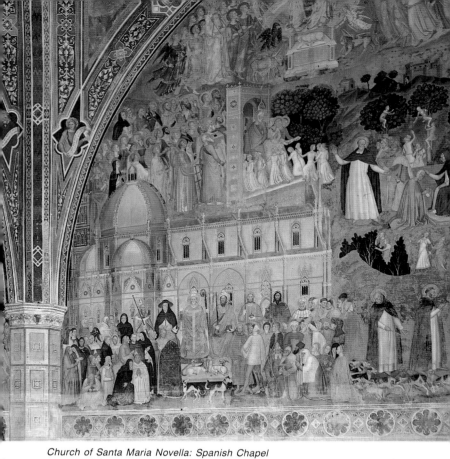

Church of Santa Maria Novella: Spanish Chapel

Church of Santa Maria Novella: cloister

greatest Florentine painters of the 15th and 16th centuries. At present it is not open to the public for it is now part of a school for Carabinieri.

Obelisks of Piazza Santa Maria Novella These two large pyramidal obelisks in marble are decorated at the top by elegant bronze lilies. In the 16th century they marked the ends of the course of the historic chariot race (*Palio dei Cocchi*).

Loggia of San Paolo This elegant little loggia is decorated with nine terracotta *roundels* by Giovanni della Robbia, and under the portico houses the *Encounter between St. Dominic and St. Francis*, another marvelous terra-cotta by Andrea della Robbia.

Church of Ognissanti (Borgo Ognissanti 42. Open: 9-12, closed holidays.) The church of Ognissanti, built in 1256, has often been reconstructed, particularly in the 17th century, and little of the original features remain.
The *facade* is by Matteo Nigetti (1639) and is one of the first examples of Baroque architecture in the city.
The spacious and well balanced *interior* has large Renaissance altars. On the second altar to the right is a fresco of the *Madonna of Mercy* by Domenico Ghirlandaio; under this is a *Deposition* also by Ghirlandaio. About the center of the right aisle is a fresco with *St. Augustine* (1480) by Botticelli, and across from it, on the left wall, Ghirlandaio's *St. Jerome* (1480). On the right, on the pavement of the chapel in the crossing, is the *tomb of Mariano Filipepi* and his children, including the great Botticelli.
The fine dome has frescoes by Giovanni da San Giovanni; in the *Sacristy* is a painted wooden *Crucifix* of the school of Giotto and a fine fresco, the *Crucifixion*, attributed to Taddeo Gaddi.
Next to the church is the *Cloister*, in the style of Michelozzo, with scenes from the *Life of St. Francis* by Iacopo Ligozzi (1625).
A door leads to the *Refectory* which contains a fine *Last Supper* by Ghirlandaio.

Cenacolo di Foligno Inside the ex Convent of S. Onofrio, of the so-called Franciscans from Foligno, the refectory contains the fresco with the *Last Supper* by Perugino and assistants (1490). In the painting, beyond Christ and the Apostles, the architecture opens out on a country scene with *Christ on the Mount of Olives*.

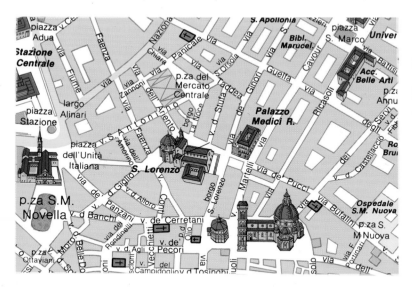

Quarter of S. Lorenzo One of the most picturesque and typical quarters of Florence, San Lorenzo winds through the piazza, dominated by the large Church of San Lorenzo, and a multitude of small narrow streets which lead to the "Mercato Centrale", the largest center for the sale of foodstuffs. Long rows of booths stretch around the large structures of the Mercato, turning the area into one of the busiest shopping centers in Florence.

Statue of Giovanni delle Bande Nere This imposing marble portrait shows the famous soldier of fortune seated and with a scepter in his hand. It is considered one of Baccio Bandinelli's best works. The sculptor also made the finely executed base (1540).

Church of San Lorenzo Consecrated by St. Ambrose in 393, it is the oldest church in the city.

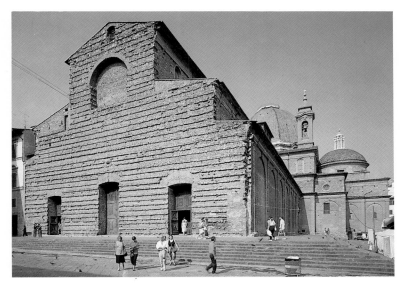

Church of San Lorenzo

It was then rebuilt along Romanesque lines in 1060. The present building dates to 1423 and was designed and built by Brunelleschi.

The simple bare **facade** lacks the marble revetment; Michelangelo's design was never carried out. The **internal facade** which Michelangelo also designed is comprised of three doors between two pilasters with garlands of oak and laurel and a balcony on two Corinthian columns.

The **interior** has a nave separated from the side aisles by Corinthian columns. The ceiling has magnificent gilded rosettes in white-ground coffering.

The second chapel of the **right aisle** contains the *Wedding of the Virgin* by Rosso Fiorentino (1523) with the brilliant coloring typical of the Mannerist painters; next to it is the Gothic *tomb slab of F. Landini*, organist, carved in 1398. After the two paintings of *St. Lawrence* and the *Adoration of the*

SAN LORENZO
1) Balcony (Michelangelo)
2) Wedding of the Virgin (Rosso Fiorentino)
3) Marble tabernacle (Desiderio da Settignano)
4-5) Bronze pulpits (Donatello)
6) Cappella Maggiore (Chancel)
7) Sacrestia Vecchia
8) Annunciation (Filippo Lippi)
9) Martyrdom of St. Lawrence (Bronzino)
10) Marble choir stall (Attrib. to Donatello)
11) Entrance to the Medici Chapels
12) Cappella dei Principi
13) Sacrestia Nuova
14) Cloister of S. Lorenzo
15) Vestibule of the Laurentian Library

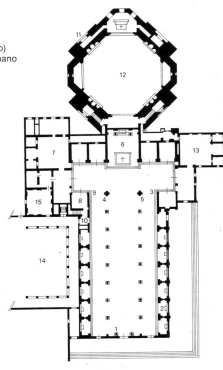

Church of San Lorenzo: interior

Magi comes the *ciborium* of 1461 by Desiderio da Settignano.
In the right-hand chapel of the transept is a Roman *sarcophagus*, reused for the burial of Niccolò Stenone; in the main chapel is a marble *Crucifix* by Baccio da Montelupo, while the central **dome** is frescoed with *Florentine Saints in Glory* by Vincenzo Meucci (1742). The left transept contains the wooden statue of the *Madonna and Child*, a polychromed late 14th-century work, the painting of *Saints* by the school of Ghirlandaio and Filippo Lippi's *Annunciation* diptych. The Annunciation dates to 1440 and has a remarkable feeling for space thanks to the three-dimensionality of the figures and the perspective sudy of the building in the background.
The *left aisle* contains the large fresco with the *Martyrdom of St. Lawrence* by Bronzino (1565-1569) and the marble *choir-loft* which may have been designed by Donatello. Under the arches of the last two bays of the nave are Donatello's two bronze *pulpits*, like two large classic arches on columns. The Dionysiac scenes which fill in the empty spaces betray their inspiration from ancient monuments. The panel executed by Donatello's pupils - Bellano and Bertoldo - include the *Crucifixion*, the *Deposition*, part of the *Passion of Christ*, *St. John the Evangelist* and the *Flagellation* on the left pulpit and the *Martyrdom of St. Lawrence*, the *Resurrection* and the other part of the *Passion* on the right pulpit.
The **Sacrestia Vecchia** or Old Sacristy at the back of the left transept was built by Brunelleschi between 1419 and 1428. Earlier than the church, the sacristy is the first example of early Renaissance architecture and of the work of Brunelleschi in Florence. A dome covers the square room and a square apse opens off one wall. The structural lines are stressed by stone molding. Eight roundels by Donatello (1435-1443) with the *Four Evangelists* and *Scenes from the Life of St. John* are set into the pendentives and the lunettes. The bronze *doors* and the stucco *reliefs* over the doors are also by Donatello, while the *funeral monument to Piero and Giovanni de' Medici* (1472) is by Andrea del Verrocchio. Andrea Cavalcanti made the *balustrade* of the apse after a design by Donatello, as well as the *sarcophagus of Giovanni Bicci de' Medici and his wife*.
On the opposite side, near the right transept of the church, is the Sacrestia Nuova with the entrance from the outside.

Medici Chapels (Piazza Madonna degli Aldobrandini. Open: 9-14, closed Monday.) This extensive complex which contains the Medici family tombs is attached to the back of the Church of San Lorenzo where it makes use of the basement quarters in addition to various other rooms.
The entrance is on the Piazza Madonna degli Aldobrandini and leads to a

Medici Chapels

mo the Elder, of *Donatello*, and of the various members of the *House of Lorraine* as well as other grand-ducal sepulchers. From here one moves up to the **Cappella dei Principi**, in part by Nigetti (Buontalenti also had a hand in the design), dating to 1602 and finished in the 18th century. From the outside the building is Baroque, with a tall windowed drum supporting a large dome faced in brick, inspired by the dome on the cathedral. The *interior* is octagonal in plan, entirely lined with pietre dure and marble in keeping with Baroque taste. The wainscotting is decorated with the *sixteen coats of arms*

Medici Chapels: Chapel of the Princes

Medici Chapels: Sacrestia Nuova. Tomb of Giuliano duke of Nemours *and* Tomb of Lorenzo duke of Urbino, *Michelangelo*

of the Tuscan grand-ducal cities. Above are the *six coffers or tombs* of the *grand dukes Cosimo III, Francesco I, Cosimo I, Ferdinando I, Cosimo II, Ferdinando II*, over two of which stand *statues of the Grand Dukes* by Tacca. Narrow rooms open off to either side of the altar. Once sacristies, they now contain a collection of *relics* and the *treasure* comprised of glass vases, church furniture and reliquaries dating to the 17th and 18th centuries. A corridor leads from the Cappella dei Principi to the **Sacrestia Nuova**.

This room, designed by Michelangelo around 1520 overturns the restrained equilibrium of Brunelleschi's room in a dynamic unrelenting rhythm of the wall decoration. Under the dome with its perspective coffering the walls of the square space are articulated by niches, pilasters and molding. Facing the tomb with the *altar* designed by Michelangelo is the *sarcophagus of Lorenzo the Magificent and Giuliano de' Medici*, above which are the statues of *St. Damian* (by Raffaello di Montelupo), the *Madonna and Child* (by Michelangelo) and *St. Cosmas* (by Giovannangelo Montorsoli). The *tombs of Giuliano, duke of Nemours*, and *of Lorenzo, duke of Urbino*, face each other at the center of the other two walls. Michelangelo placed the sarcophaguses with the reclining *Allegories of Time* under the statues of the dukes set in niches: Giuliano's tomb is watched over by *Day* and *Night* while *Dusk* and *Dawn* watch over Lorenzo's. The accurate anatomical depiction of the figures, which are in part unfinished, expresses the intrinsic meaning through exterior form and here Michelangelo created one of his greatest masterpieces.

Medici Chapels: Sacrestia Nuova. Madonna and Child, *Michelangelo;* St. Damian, *Raffaello da Montelupo;* St. Cosma, *Giovannangelo Montorsoli.*

Medici Chapels: Sacrestia Nuova. *Day and Dawn, Michelangelo*

Palazzo Medici-Riccardi: Chapel. Journey of the Three Magi to Bethlehem, *Benozzo Gozzoli*

Palazzo Medici-Riccardi The palace that Cosimo the Elder had built as his official family residence - the first Renaissance example - is by Michelozzo. The building as he originally built it between 1444 and 1464 was shorter than what we see now; not until 1517 was the open arched loggia on the ground floor filled in, and the «kneeling» *gabled windows* attributed to Michelangelo were added. When the palace was bought by the Riccardi, the facade was lengthened between 1600 and 1700 and the inner building was enlarged, changing the aspect of the original project.

On the exterior the building is a powerful construction with rusticated ashlars on the ground floor and the arcades in smooth ashlars; above the dentellated cornice moldings of classic inspiration, Michelozzo raised the upper stories with each stage smoother than the preceding one; the first floor is thus in smooth ashlars and the second in flat finely fitted blocks of stone. The windows of the upper stories are two-light windows with a roundel over the column, inscribed in round arches; the palace is crowned by a bracketed cornice obviously inspired by antiquity.

Inside is the ***First Courtyard*** with arcades and a series of two-light openings and a loggia, decorated with 15th-centurys *graffiti* by Maso di Bartolomeo and *roundels* by Bertoldo. Various antique works of art are to be found in the courtyard with, in front of the entrance, *Orpheus* by Baccio Bandinelli. Entrance to the ***Chapel***, by Michelozzo, is through the courtyard.

The ceiling is coffered and there is an inlaid floor (1465). The *Arrival of the Magi in Bethlehem* unfolds on the walls. In this fresco Benozzo Gozzoli (1459-60) painted portraits of the personages present at the Council of Florence in 1439 (John VII, Lorenzo, Piero the Gouty with his daughters, Galeazzo Maria Sforza, Sigismondo Malatesta, as well as Benozzo himself and Fra Angelico can be recognized).

The palazzo also contains the *Gallery*, a 17th-century hall with stuccoes, the vault of which was frescoed by Luca Giordano with the *Apotheosis of the Medici Dynasty* (1682) surrounded by various mythological allegories.

This gallery communicates with the ***Biblioteca Riccardiana***, with its wealth of volumes, manuscripts and incunabulae; the vault of the Exhibition Hall is decorated with the fresco of *Intellect Released from the Bonds of Ignorance*, by Luca Giordano (1683).

AREA OF GALLERIA DELL'ACCADEMIA

Galleria dell'Accademia - **Church and Convent of San Marco** - Museum of Geology and Palaeontology - Botanical Museum - Museum of Mineralogy - **Piazza and Church of SS. Annunziata** - Galleria and Ospedale degli Innocenti - **Archaeological Museum** - Cenacolo of Sant'Apollonia - Cloister of the Scalzo

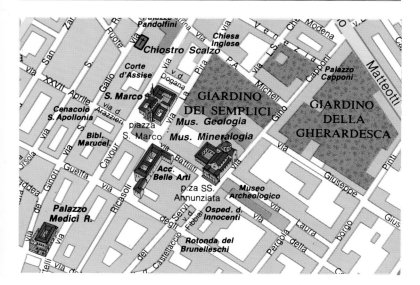

Galleria dell'Accademia (Via Ricasoli 60. Open: 9-14, holid. 9-13, closed Mondays.) The Gallery houses an extremely important collection of sculpture by Michelangelo. The *room* that leads to the tribune, hung with tapestries, contains the *Palestrina Pietà*, whose attribution to Michelangelo is controversial, the unfinished *St. Matthew*, made for the Florentine cathedral ,and the four «*Prisons*» (or slaves) which were meant for the tomb of Julius II in St. Peter's in Rome, which was never finished, like these male figures who seem to be trying to free themselves from the marble grip.

At the center of the spacious ***Tribune*** is the original of the *David* (1501-4) commissioned from the great sculptor to replace Donatello's *Judith* on the

Galleria dell'Accademia: Palestrina Pietà *and* St. Matthew, *Michelangelo*

balustrade of the Palazzo dei Priori. The room also contains an important collection of *paintings* of the Tuscan school of the 13th and 14th centuries. Three *small rooms* are to the right of the Tribune and contain various *shrines* attributed to Bernardo Daddi and a fine *Pietà* by Giovanni da Milano. To the left another series of three *small rooms* contains works by famous masters of the 14th century: of note are a fine *Polyptych* by Andrea Orcagna, and two series of panels representing scenes from the *Life of Christ* and *Scenes from the Life of St. Francis*, by Taddeo Gaddi. To the left of the Tribune there is another large *hall* containing works of the Florentine 15th century, including Lorenzo Monaco's *Annunciation*, Filippino Lippi's *St. John the Baptist and the Magdalen*, the *Madonna of the Sea*, attributed either to Botticelli or Filippino Lippi, and a fine *panel from a wedding chest*, known as the *Adimari wedding chest*, by an unknown Florentine painter of the 15th century.

Church and Convent of San Marco (Piazza S. Marco 1. Open: 9-14, holid. 9-13, closed Mondays.) The Convent was mentioned as early as the 12th century. In 1437 Cosimo the Elder commissioned Michelozzo to rebuild it and the convent of San Marco was therefore the first to be built in the elegant terse forms of the Renaissance.

The fine **Cloister** is a simple stone structure with brick cornices. Light arcades delimit the space on the ground floor. On the first floor are fine *lunettes* frescoed by Pocetti, Rosselli, Coccapani, Vanni, Cerrini, Dandini and other illustrious artists. But most of the frescoes in the cloister are by Fra Angelico who passed the greater part of his life within these walls; his works include: *Crucifixion with St. Dominic* at the entrance to the cloister and the lunette over the door with *St. Peter Martyr*; in the lunette of the *Chapter Room*, a *St. Dominic*, and inside a magnificent *Crucifixion*; over the door of the refectory a *Pietà*; on the door of the Hospice, *Jesus as a Pilgrim* and, inside, the *Madonna dell'Arte dei Lanaioli* (1433) the *Last Judgement, Scenes from the Life of Christ*, the *Deposition*. In the Refectory a fine *Supper of St. Dominic*, a fresco by Sogliani, and on the walls the *Last Judgement* by Fra Bartolomeo. A staircase leads to the next floor with Fra Angelico's famous *Annunciation* at the top; off the corridor is the splendid **Library** by Michelozzo and at the end of the corridor, the **Cell** used by **Cosimo de' Medici** with a *Crucifix* in the ante-chamber and an *Adoration of the Magi* in the cell, both by Fra Angelico. In the left corridor one can admire an *Enthroned Madonna between Saints* and in the cells that open off the corridor, other lovely works, all by Fra Angelico: the *Annunciation*, the *Transfiguration*, *Christ before the Praetor*, the *Maries at the Tomb*, the *Coronation*, the *Presentation in the Temple*. At the end of the corridor is **Savonarola's cell** where there is a portrait of the martyr painted by Fra Bartolomeo. A flight of stairs on the right leads down to the **Small Refectory** with a large fresco of the *Last Supper* by Ghirlandaio.

The **Salone dell'Ospizio** or Hospice contains a number of panel paintings; particular note should be taken of Fra Angelico's *Last Judgement* and his *Deposition*.

The **Church** was restored in 1437 by Michelozzo himself; it was later remodeled by Giambologna (1580) and then by Silvani; the simple facade was redone between 1777 and 1780.

The **interior** is linear and the carved and gilded ceiling is of note. On the door is a *Crucifix* of the school of Giotto, while works on the altars include, on the right, *St. Thomas Aquinas* by Santi di Tito and a *Praying Madonna* of Byzantine school.

Nearby is Michelozzo's **Sacristy** which contains a *sarcophagus* with a bronze statue of *St. Antoninus* by Fra Domenico Portigiani (1602).

Nearby is the **Chapel of St. Antoninus** with marble and bronze decorations by Giambologna and Francavilla, and other works by Alessandro Allori and Battista Naldini; the *frescoes* in the dome are by Poccetti.

To the left of the presbytery note should be taken of the lovely **Cappella del Sacramento** decorated with *frescoes* by Poccetti and *canvasas* by Santi di Tito, Passignano and Empoli.

Museum of Geology and Paleontology (Via G. La Pira 4. Open: Mondays 14-18, Thursdays and Saturdays 9-13, first Sunday of the month 9.30-12.30). The current arrangement dates back to the beginning of the century. Of outstanding note the extensive collection of vertebrates and fossil finds from the Valdarno. On the second floor there are thousands of examples of invertebrates.

Galleria dell'Accademia: David, Michelangelo

Convent of San Marco: Ante-cella of Girolamo Savonarola

Botanical Museum (Via G. La Pira 4. Open: Mondays, Wednesdays, Fridays 9-12, the first Sunday of the month 9-12. Botanical Gardens "Giardino dei Semplici" - Via Micheli 3. Open: Mondays, Wednesdays, Fridays 9-12). This is one of the largest in the peninsula and one of the best-known museums of its kind in the world. Included are the *Erbario centrale* (1842) which boasts of about four million specimens. An interesting *Tropical herbarium* and a *Xylotheque* adjacent to the museum are the *Botanical Gardens* founded in 1545 at the behest of Cosimo I de' Medici, which contain extremely rare tall trees.

Museo di Mineralogia (Via G. La Pira 4. Open: 9-12, Wednesday also 15-18.) The Mineralogy Museum is an enormous collection of over 25,000 samples of minerals from all over the world which was begun by Cosimo I de' Medici. The *Elbana Collection* (5000 pieces) is particularly interesting. Exceptional pieces include a Brazilian topaz weighing 151 kilos, the Elba tourmalines and the Sardinian azurites.

Church of SS. Annunziata When it was originally built (1250) it was an oratory outside the second circle of walls. As time went on, the church was enlarged until it assumed its present size.
Entrance to the church is through the so-called *Chiostrino dei Voti* built by Antonio Manetti after designs by Michelozzo (1447). The space is remarkably scenographic with lunettes frescoed with scenes from the *Life of the Virgin* including (from the right) works of high quality such as the *Assumption* (1513) by Rosso Fiorentino, the *Visitation* (1513) by Pontormo, the *Marriage of the Virgin* (1513), the *Birth of the Virgin* and the *Voyage of the Magi* (1511) by Andrea del Sarto.
The Chiostrino is also decorated with *Scenes from the Life of St. Filippo Benizzi* by Cosimo Rosselli, the *Punishment of the Blasphemer*, the *Healing of a Man Possessed*, the *Resurrection of a Child*, the *Healing of a Child*, by Andrea del Sarto.
The *interior*, remodeled in the middle of the 17th century, consists of a single majestic nave. Between the pilasters on either side arches lead to the chapels; the church is enriched by the magnificent coffered *ceiling* by Volterrano (1664). The large *tribune* of the choir, with a hemispherical *cupola* designed by Leon Battista Alberti (1444), is also particularly fine.
To the left of the entrance is the *Tabernacle of the Annunciata* by Michelozzo, built around a 14th-century fresco of the *Annunciation* traditionally considered miraculous. The tabernacle consists of four Corinthian columns with a rich entablature; the *dome* is by Volterrano, the *gate*, in bronze ropes, is by Maso di Bartolomeo (1447), the silver *altar* is by Egidio Leggi (1600).
Rossellino's *funerary monument to Orlando de' Medici* is in the fifth chapel on the right; the chapel to the left of the right transept contains the *tomb*

Church of the SS. Annunziata

of Baccio Bandinelli with his *Pietà*.
Near the Presbytery at the center is the **Giambologna Chapel** which the
sculptor transformed for his own burial (1598).
Michelozzo's terra-cotta statue of *John the Baptist* is at the back of the left
transept; the fourth chapel of the left side is decorated with an *Assumption*
by Perugino, while the first two chapels contain important frescoes by Andrea del Castagno - *Christ with St. Julian* and the *Trinity with St. Jerome between the Madonna and Mary of Cleofa*.
A door from the left arm of the transept leads to the **Chiostro dei Morti**,

Church of the SS. Annunziata: interior

Piazza of the SS. Annunziata: Equestrian statue of Ferdinando I de' Medici, Giambologna, and Ospedale degli Innocenti

designed by Michelozzo (1453) and decorated with a fresco cycle of the *History of the Order of the Servi* attributed to Maria di Bernardino Poccetti; the series is interrupted in the arch of the portal of the church by Andrea del Sarto's *Madonna del Sacco.* On the wall which abuts on the church note should be taken of the *tomb of Guglielmo di Narbona,* who fell in the battle of Campaldino, for it furnishes rare evidence of the battle armor of a knight at the end of the 13th century.

Fountains by Tacca The two fountains are symmetrically placed at either side of the piazza. They were made by Pietro Tacca (1629) for the port of Leghorn (Livorno) but Grand Duke Ferdinando II had them installed in the Florentine piazza. The two bronze fountains are decidedly 16th-century in style and reproduce marine monsters and grotesques of outstanding artistic quality.

Galleria dell'Ospedale degli Innocenti The five rooms of this small museum contain important works of the 15th and 16th centuries including the splendid *Adoration of the Christ Child,* with the sweet serene figures of the worshippers, by Ghirlandaio (1488), the *Madonna and Child* (1488) in terracotta by Luca della Robbia; the famous *Madonna and Child with St. John* (1460) by Botticelli, and an imposing *Madonna and Saints* by Pietro di Cosimo.

Ospedale degli Innocenti (Foundling Home) (Piazza SS. Annunziata 12. Open: 9-14, holid. 9-13, closed Wednesdays.) Designed by Brunelleschi, the building was finished by Francesco Luna (1445). A lovely portico runs along the facade. Its nine arcades are decorated with polychrome terra-cotta roundels of *Infants in Swaddling Clothes,* by Luca della Robbia (1463). Inside is a lovely courtyard and there are two collections on the first floor.

Loggia of the Confraternita dei Servi di Maria Right opposite the Ospedale degli Innocenti, the loggia echoes its portico. It was built by Antonio da Sangallo the Elder and Baccio d'Agnolo in 1516.

Archaeological Museum (Via della Colonna 36. Open: 9-14, holid. 9-13, closed Mondays.) One of the most important museums of its kind in Italy for the wealth of its collections which include examples of Egyptian, Etruscan, Greek and Roman antiquities.

The *Egyptian Collection* was begun in 1824 at the behest of Leopoldo II and was enriched by material from Tuscan expeditions directed by Ippolito Rossellini. Some of the most interesting items include the striking statue of the *goddess Hathor nursing the Pharaoh*, the polychrome relief of the *goddess Hathor with the Pharaoh, Sethos I*, the bas-relief of the *goddess of Truth Maat* and the *funerary statue of the priest Amenemhet*.

The *Etruscan section* comprises an immense amount of material collected in over three centuries of study. There are a great number of sarcophagi, cinerary urns, bronzes, weapons and objects of daily use. Particularly striking in the field of sculpture are the famous *Chimaera*, the staue of the orator known as the *Arringatore*, and the statue of *Minerva*.

The *Graeco-Roman section*, even though considerably smaller, includes very important pieces such as the bronze statue konwn as *Idolino*, a Greek work of the 5th century B.C.

Of great interest is the vast *Collection of vases and terracottas* of Italic, Etruscan and Greek make (including the famous *François Vase*, a Greek work of the 6th century B.C. found in an Etruscan tomb), as well as the sections of *Eastern Mediterranean culture, Prehistory* and rooms with the *copies of the frescoes from the Etruscan tombs of Orvieto*.

The annexed *Garden* contains various reconstructions of tombs of the Etruscan period using the original material, a model of a small temple and other antique architectural elements.

Cenacolo di Santa Apollonia (Via XXVII Aprile. Open: weekd. 9-14, holid. 9-13, closed Mondays.) This small well-preserved building houses the evocative and famous fresco of the *Last Supper* by Andrea del Castagno (1457). Note also on the left wall three scenes with the *Crucifixion*, the *Deposition* and the *Resurrection*, also by Andrea. In the two lunettes are a *Pietà* and a *Crucifixion with the Virgin, St. John and Saints*, by an unknown painter.

Chiostro dello Scalzo (Via Cavour 69.) Site of an old confraternity - the Scalzo - this well-balanced and elegant little cloister contains stupendous monochrome frescoes which recount sixteen stories from the *Life of St. John the Baptist*. The frescoes are all by Andrea del Sarto (1514-26) except two which are by Franciabigio (1518-19).

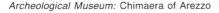

Archeological Museum: Chimaera of Arezzo

AREA OF ## SANTA CROCE

Church of Santa Croce - **Museum of the Opera di Santa Croce** - Casa
Buonarroti - Church of Sant'Ambrogio - Church of Santa Maria Maddalena dei Pazzi - Museo di Firenze com'era

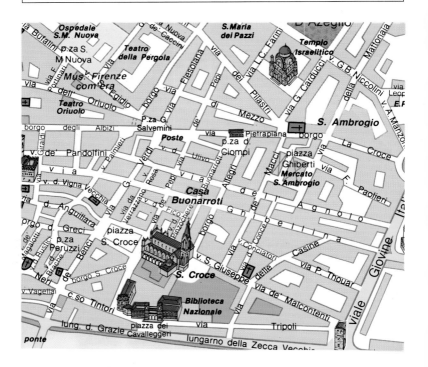

Piazza Santa Croce. This vast rectangular piazza is one of the largest in
the city. Dominated by the imposing structure of the Church of S. Croce, it
is surrounded by historical palaces.
During the Middle Ages it was considered the ideal place for meetings and
preaching.
In the Renaissance it was used for tournaments and then became the stage
for the football matches (calcio storico fiorentino) which are still today played
here.

Church of Santa Croce The church is one of city's largest and has a neo-
Gothic *facade* added on in the 19th century with a heavy superabundance
of ornamentation. The building, attributed to Arnolfo di Cambio, has a majestic *interior* where the nave is separated from the two aisles by slender octagonal piers which support the broad pointed arches with a double molding.
At the end of the nave, with its open timber roof, is the transept with a number of chapels . The internal wall of the facade contains a stained-glass roundel with the *Deposition*, done on a cartoon by Lorenzo Ghiberti. Below on
the right is the *monument to Gino Capponi* by Antonio Bortone (1876) while
on the left is the *monument to G.B. Niccolini*, historian and poet, by Pio Fedi.
On the first altar in the **right aisle** is a *Crucifixion* by Santi di Tito (1579),
while the famous *Madonna del Latte*, a bas-relief by Antonio Rossellino, is
on the first pier. On the wall are the *funeral monuments to Michelangelo
Buonarroti*, by Vasari (1564), *to Vittorio Alfieri*, poet and patriot, by Canova
(1803), and *to Niccolò Machiavelli* by Innocenzo Spinazzi (1787). The octagonal pulpit by Benedetto da Maiano (1477), a sculptural ensemble with
Scenes from the Life of St. Francis, is at the third pier. Behind the fifth altar
are remains of frescoes by Andrea Orcagna, while further on is a tabernacle
in *pietra serena* with the *Annunciation* by Donatello (1472-76), a particularly
rich example of a monument; the *tomb* of the historian *Leonardo Bruni*, by
Rossellino; the *funeral monument to Gioacchino Rossini* and the one to the
poet *Ugo Foscolo* by Antonio Berti (1939).

Church of Santa Croce

In the **Castellani Chapel** or «*Chapel of the Sacrament*», in the right arm of the transept, is the cycle of frescoes with scenes from the *Lives of SS. Nicholas of Bari, Anthony Abbot, John the Evangelist and John the Baptist*, by Agnolo Gaddi (1385); a fine *crucifix* by Niccolò Gerini is at the altar while on the walls are terra-cotta *Saints* from the Della Robbia workshop. Further on, at the head of the transept, is the **Baroncelli Chapel**. Outside is the magnificent *tomb* in Gothic style of the Baroncelli family and a lunette with a *Madonna* by Taddeo Gaddi. Inside, on the right wall, the fine fresco of the *Madonna of the Girdle with St. Thomas*, by Bastiano Mainardi (1490) and the cycle of *Scenes from the Life of Mary*, by Taddeo Gaddi, on the other three walls; on the altar is the fine *Coronation of the Virgin* by Giotto.

Michelozzo's portal in the right side of the transept leads to the **Sacristy**, originally built in the 14th century, and with *Scenes from the Passion* by Niccolò Gerini on the right wall.

SANTA CROCE

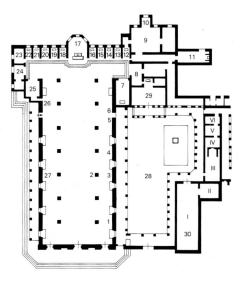

Church of Santa Croce. Opposite, top to bottom: interior; Funeral Monument to Michelangelo, *Vasari;* Funeral monument to Galileo Galilei, *Foggini;* Funeral monument to Vittorio Alfieri, *Canova;* Funeral monument to Dante Alighieri, *Ricci.* Above: Bardi Chapel

In the central or east wall of the Sacristy is the **Rinuccini Chapel** with scenes from the *Lives of the Virgin and St. Mary Magdalen* by Giovanni da Milano and a fine *altarpiece* by Giovanni del Biondo (1379). The Sacristy also leads to the **Medici Chapel** or «*Novices' Chapel*», built by Michelozzo for Cosimo the Elder.

Various Della Robbia pieces here include *busts* as well as an *altarpiece* and a *shrine* by Verrocchio; to the right is the *monument to Francesco Lombardi* with a magnificent bas-relief that may be by Donatello.

Various chapels with important works of art open off the back of the central part of the transept: the **Velluti Chapel** with *Scenes from the Legend of St. Michael Archangel*, perhaps by Cimabue; the **Bellacci Chapel** with a lunette-shaped vault with *Scenes from the Life of St. Andrew Apostle* by Giovanni da San Giovanni; the **Silvestri Chapel** with the *monument to Carlotta Buonaparte*, by Lorenzo Bartolini; the **Peruzzi Chapel** with the magnificent *Scenes from the Life of St. John Evangelist* by Giotto (1320); the **Bardi Chapel** with the *Scenes from the Life of St. Francis* by Giotto (1318) and, above the external arch, the *Miracle of the Stigmata*, while the *Allegory of Chastity, Poverty* and *Obedience*, and the *Triumph of the Saint* were frescoed on the vaulting by Giotto.

On the altar is a panel of *St. Francis* and *Scenes from his Life* of Luccan school, late 13th century; then comes the **Chancel (Cappella Maggiore)** with the *Legend of the True Cross* (1380) by Agnolo Gaddi. On the altar is a polyptych with the *Madonna* and *Saints* by Niccolò Gerini and above the altar a *Crucifixion* or Triumphal Cross, of the school of Giotto; next comes the **Tosinghi Chapel** with, on the altar, a *polyptych* by Giovanni del Biondo; the **Benci Chapel** with the *monument to the Virgin Mary and her Dead Son* by Libero Andreotti (1926); the **Ricasoli Chapel**, with two 19th-century can-

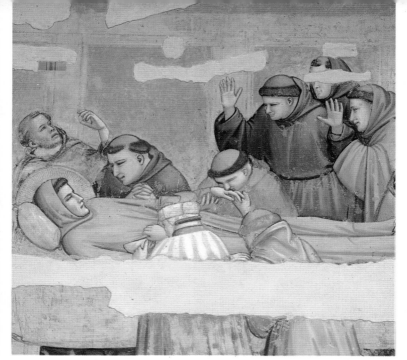

Church of Santa Croce. Opposite: Cappella Maggiore (Chancel).
Above: Bardi Chapel. Funeral of Saint Francis, *Giotto*

vases of *Scenes from the Life of St. Anthony of Padua*; the **Pulci Chapel** with a glazed terra-cotta *altarpiece* by Giovanni della Robbia and noteworthy frescoes on the walls (the *Martyrdom of SS Lawrence and Stephen* by Bernardo Daddi); the **Bardi di Vernio Chapel** frescoed with scenes from the *Life of Pope Sylvester* (by Giottino) and with two niche-shaped 14th-century *tombs* on the left wall.

At the far end of the left arm of the crossing are the **Niccolini Chapel** with *statues* by Pietro Francavilla, *paintings* by Alessandro Allori (1588) on the altars and a fine *cupola* frescoed by Volterrano (1660); the **Bardi Chapel** (the last to the left of the crossing) with Donatello's magnificent *Crucifix* (1425), and the **Salviati Chapel**, with the *Martyrdom of St. Lawrence* by Jacopo Ligozzi (1600) on the altar.

The *tombs* of the humanist *Carlo Marsuppini* by Desiderio da Settignano, and *Galileo Galilei* (1642) by Foggini are in the **left aisle**.

Access to the **First Cloister** outside the right side of the church is through the *Porta del Martello* to the right of the facade. The 14th-century cloister is articulated by fine arcades.

At the back of the cloister is the marvelous **Pazzi Chapel** which Brunelleschi designed on a central plan with a dome and a lantern. Outside, a classicizing Corinthian porch is set in front of the facade, with a *frieze* containing roundels with heads of cherubim, designed by Donatello and executed by Desiderio da Settignano. A fine *door* designed by Giuliano da Maiano (1472) opens on one of the long sides of the rectangular interior. The ribbed *dome* and lantern are set above the walls articulated by pilasters.

A door in the right-hand corner of the First Cloister, by Michelozzo or Benedetto da Maiano, opens into the **Second Cloister**, or *Large Cloister*, designed by Brunelleschi and probably decorated by Rossellino. Entrance to the former *Refectory* and the **Museo dell'Opera di Santa Croce** is on the right of the first cloister.

Museo dell'Opera di Santa Croce (Piazza S. Croce 16. Open: summer 10-12.30; 14.30-18.30; winter 10-12.30; 15-17; closed Wednesdays.)

Installed to one side of the Church, the museum consists of six rooms in what used to be the convent. The entrance room contains a fine fresco, *Saint Francis distributing Bread to the Friars*, by Jacopo Ligozzi. The door on the right leads into a large hall (the old **Refectory**) dominated by a large fresco by Taddeo Gaddi with the *Tree of Life, a Last Supper* and various *Episodes from the Life of Christ*. The room also contains Cimabue's famous *Crucifix* which

Museo dell'Opera di Santa Croce: Crucifix, *Cimabue*

was so heavily damaged in the flood of 1966, a bronze statue of *St. Louis of Toulouse* by Donatello and detached frescoes by Andrea del Giusto, Domenico Veneziano and other anonymous Florentine painters.

Back in the entrance hall, the doorway to the left leads to a room (the old **Cappella Cerchi**) in which various outstanding Della Robbia *terra cottas* are on display, in particular a glazed terra-cotta *altarpiece* attributed to Andrea della Robbia, a *Madonna and Child* of the school of the Della Robbias, and over the door, a *predella* of fine quality, also by Andrea. Of note in the next room are two *Busts of Saints*, which emerged from under the intonaco in the Pazzi Chapel; a fine detached fresco depicting the *Martyrdom of St. Matthew*, by the school of Andrea del Castagno; a delightful *Madonna Enthroned*, perhaps by Pietro Gerini; the fresco with the *Madonna of Humility*, probably from the circle of Lorenzo Monaco, and other interesting frescoes, mostly from the Basilica. Of particular note in the next room is the *funeral monument of Cardinal Gastone della Torre* by the great Tino di Camaino. And finally the particularly striking works in the last room include two spandrels with *Angels* attributed to Matteo Rosselli, a detached fresco depicting *Christ in the Garden*, also by Rosselli, and another detached fresco of *Christ in the Garden* and the *Apparition of Christ to the Madonna*, of the school of Giovanni da San Giovanni.

Casa Buonarroti (Via Ghibellina 70. Open weekd. 10-14, holid. 9-13) Bought by Michelangelo himself in 1508 for his nephew Leonardo, it was later frescoed in the 17th century at the request and under the guidance of Michelangelo the Younger. Here the principal 17th-century Florentine painters frescoed a rich cycle of paintings with the *Glories of Michelangelo*. Today the building contains the **Museum** of Michelangelo's early works.

Church of Sant'Ambrogio Sant'Ambrogio was one of the first religious buildings to go up in Florence. Rebuilt in the 13th century and again more recently, the present **facade** is 19th century.

The **interior**, 18th-century on an originally Gothic ground plan, is single-

Museo dell'Opera di Santa Croce: refectory

aisled with three chapels at the back and eight Renaissance *side altars*. There were originally a group of 14th- and 15th-century *frescoes* near the altars but they were seriously damaged in the flood of 1966 and were therefore detached. Near the Presbytery is the **Cappella del Miracolo** with a 15th-century *Tabernacle of the Holy Sacrament* which contains the blood which miraculously appeared in the chalice of a priest, Uguccione, as he was celebrating Mass. The *tabernacle* which contains the reliquary is by Mino da Fiesole (1481-83); the *angels* nearby in terracotta are by the Della Robbia while the *frescoes* on the walls are 15th-century paintings by Cosimo Roselli.

Church of Santa Maria Maddalena dei Pazzi This church and the Benedictine monastery connected with it, were first built in the 13th century; the buildings were often remodeled, especially between 1480 and 1492 by Giuliano da Sangallo. Entrance to the church is through the **Cappella del Giglio**, a 16th-century structure frescoed by Poccetti with scenes from the *Lives of SS. Nereo, Achilleo, Bernard and Filippo Neri*, and the annexed *courtyard*, with an Ionic portico, by Sangallo.
The **interior** of the church has a single aisle and six arches on either side lead into the chapels which contain various distinguished works of the 16th and 17th centuries. The **Cappella Maggiore** has two canvases with *Scenes from the Life of the Magdalen* by Luca Giordano, set below the *dome* frescoed by Dandini.
The *crypt* at the back of the church leads to the **Chapter Hall** which contains Perugino's fresco with *Christ on the Cross and the Magdalen, St. Bernard and St. Mary, John the Baptist and St. Benedict*.

Museo di Firenze com'era (Via dell'Oriuolo 24. Open: 9-14, holid. 8-13, closed Thursdays.) Historical and topographical documents of the city, including water-colors, prints and drawings, are included in the museum of Florence as it was. In the building there is also a **Permanent exhibition of the works of Ottone Rosai**. Over fifty examples give us a survey of this great Florentine painter's artistic activity from 1930 to 1940.

Synagogue: exterior and interior

Synagogue The Israelite Temple, in an eastern Byzantine style, was designed by the architects Falcini, Treves, Micheli and Cioni (1874). When the large dome was finally covered with copper, it was inaugurated in October of 1882. The construction is interesting both for the elegant frescoes and mosaics which decorate it inside and out, and for its historical and cultural meaning. It is the symbol of the liberation from the ghetto.

AREA OF PIAZZALE MICHELANGELO

Viale dei Colli and Piazzale Michelangelo - Church of San Miniato - Forte di Belvedere

Viale dei Colli and Piazzale Michelangelo The *Viale dei Colli* (Hill Avenue) winds for about six kilometers on the heights around the south side of the city, providing panoramic spots with fascinating views. It was laid out in 1868 by the architect Giuseppe Poggi who also made the plans for the *Piazzale Michelangelo*, an enormous terrace overlooking Florence. In the piazzale are copies of Michelangelo's sculptures: *David* and the four *allegorical figures* on the Medici tombs in the New Sacristy of San Lorenzo. In the background, set above the piazzale, is the *Palazzina del Caffè* (1873), also by Poggi, which partly conceals the churches of S. Salvatore and S. Miniato al Monte.

Church of San Miniato The Church of San Miniato al Monte, which originated as a chapel in the 4th century, owes its present structure to Bishop Hildebrand (1018).

Piazzale Michelangelo: Group with the David, *copies after Michelangelo*

Church of San Miniato

The lower part of the **facade** is decorated with fine arches; the upper part is simpler and has a fine 12th-century mosaic with *Christ between the Madonna and St. Miniato.*

The **inside** is tripartite with a trussed timber ceiling. The inlaid marble pavement, with *signs of the zodiac* and *symbolic animals*, is of particular note. On the walls are fragments of 13th- and 14th-century frescoes.

The large **crypt** is closed by a *wrought-iron gate* of 1338. The *altar* (11th cent.) preserves the bones of St. Miniato; fragments of *frescoes* by Taddeo Gaddi (1341) are on the vault.

Returning from the crypt note should be taken of the raised **Presbytery**, which has a fine *pulpit* (1207) and inlaid wooden *choir stalls.*

In the conch of the apse is a large mosaic of *Christ between Mary and St. Miniato* (1277). To the right of the presbytery is the entrance to the **Sacristy**, completely frescoed by Spinello Aretino (1387) with sixteen *Scenes from the Legend of St. Benedict.*

Church of San Miniato: crypt and interior

Church of San Miniato: Sacristy, Stories of the Legend
of Saint Benedict, *Spinello Aretino*

Descending on the left of the presbytery one arrives at the **Chapel of St. Jacopo**, known as the «*Chapel of the Cardinal of Portugal*», designed by Antonio Manetti and decorated with five marvelous roundels by Luca della Robbia with the *Holy Spirit* and the *Four Cardinal Virtues*. The painting over the altar is a copy of a painting by Pietro del Pollaiolo now in the Uffizi. At the center of the church is the **Cappella del Crocifisso**, designed by Michelozzo, with a delicate vault with glazed terra-cotta decor by Luca della Robbia.

Forte di Belvedere The Forte di Belvedere, or of St. George, was commissioned from Buontalenti (1590-95) by Ferdinando I. The building, set on a hilltop south of the Arno, dominates the city and the river from within its star-shaped fortifying wall. The protected access rises through an entrance hall to the terrace in front of the **Palazzetto** which is now used for exhibitions and art manifestations. An opening in the bastions communicates with the **Boboli Gardens** below.

Forte di Belvedere

AREA OF   # PALAZZO PITTI

Palazzo Pitti - Galleria d'Arte Moderna - **Museo degli Argenti** - Museo delle Porcellane - Contini-Bonacossi Collection - **Boboli Gardens** - Museo della Specola - Church of Santa Felicita - Church of Santo Spirito - **Church of Santa Maria del Carmine**

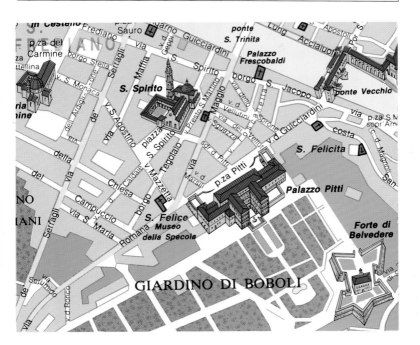

Palazzo Pitti (Piazza Pitti. Open: 9-14, holid. 9-13, closed Mondays.) Palazzo Pitti is the most imposing of the city palaces and dates to 1457 on a probable design by Brunelleschi; in the 16th century the Medicis commissioned Ammannati to enlarge it.

The *facade*, 205 meters long and 36 meters high, consists of rusticated ashlars with some of the single blocks over two meters long. The only decorative elements are the crowned heads of lions between the ground floor window brackets.

Access to the *interior* is through the great portal with its central arch which leads into a charming Doric atrium by Pasquale Poccianti (1850).

This leads to Ammannati's famous *courtyard*, at the back of which is the *Grotto of Moses*, carved in porphyry by Raffaelle Curradi; antique Roman statues are set under the arcades at the sides, while to the right is the *Chapel* frescoed by Ademollo, with a magnificent *altar* of inlaid pietra dura work and a fine *Crucifix* by Giambologna.

The *scalone d'onore*, lined with antique busts, begins on the same side of the courtyard; on the landing is the *Medici Genius* by Giambologna; the first floor goes to the vestibule of the *Royal Quarters* and the *Galleria Palatina*. On the second floor is the *Galleria d'Arte Moderna*.

The portico in the right wing of the facade of the palace leads to the *Bacchus Courtyard*, the current main entrance to the Galleria Palatina and the *Museo degli Argenti*, with the *fountain of Bacchus* by Cioli, which portrays the court dwarf of Cosimo I.

Palazzo Pitti

Palatine Gallery The Palatine Gallery is the second museum in the city, both for size and interest, after the Uffizi, and it contains works of art that are enormously important for the history of art. It was constituted by Ferdinando II de' Medici who commissioned Pietro da Cortona to decorate various rooms of the Gallery. As time passed, the collection - a typically 17th-century picture gallery with the walls entirely covered with pictures in keeping with the taste of the times - was enlarged by Cardinal Leopoldo de' Medici and, later, by the last members of the Medici family and by the Lorraine Grand Dukes. The Gallery consists of a series of rooms dedicated to gods and mythological figures represented in the decoration.

The visit begins with the **Castagnoli Room** (decorated by Castagnoli, 1784) which contains Sodoma's *Saint Sebastian*, with the saint mystically meditating on his suffering. Turning right you will find yourself in the **Volterrano Apartments**, dedicated to the painter who frescoed the five *Allegories* on the walls. Next come the **Fine Arts Room**, the **Hercules Room**, the **Aurora Room**, the **Berenice Room** and the **Room of Psyche**, which house works by Tuscan 17th-century painters. Continuing straight ahead from the Castagnoli Room we enter the **Music Room** with frescoes by Luigi Ademollo; then to the **Poccetti Gallery** (frescoes by Poccetti) which contains paintings by

Palatine Gallery: Hall of Saturn

84

Palatine Gallery: Madonna del Granduca *and* La Velata, *Raphael*

Palatine Gallery: The Four Philosophers, *Rubens*

Palatine Gallery: Virgin and Child, *Filippo Lippi*

Rubens and Spagnoletto among others, and then to the **Prometheus Room** (ceiling by Giuseppe Collignon, 1842) with an outstanding three-dimensional *Madonna* by Filippo Lippi. From here, keeping to the right, we come to the **Gallery of the Columns**, with many works by Flemish painters on the walls; then to the **Hall of Justice**, which contains the *Portrait of a Man* by Titian and various intense *Portraits* by Bronzino, and lastly to the **Room of Flora**. Back in the Prometheus Room we continue our itinerary with the **Ulysses Room**, which contains Raphael's famous *Madonna dell'Impannata*, Andrea del Sarto's *Madonna and Child with Saints* and other important paintings; on to the **Education of Jupiter Room** in which Caravaggio's famous *Sleeping Cupid* is to be found; the lovely **Iliad Room** (decoration by Luigi Sabatelli, 1819) where various authentic masterpieces are on exhibit, including one of Raphael's most famous pictures, the *Portrait of a Woman* known as *La Gravida* (1508), Andrea del Sarto's mystical *Assumption of the Virgin* (1519), the *Portrait of a Woman* by Ridolfo del Ghirlandaio, Titian's intense introspective *Portrait of a Man* and his *Philip II of Spain*, and the *Portrait of Philip IV of Spain* by Velazquez. The **Saturn Room** (ceiling by Ciro Ferri) contains works by Raphael, including the *Portraits of Angelo and Maddalena Doni*, the austere *Portrait of Cardinal Bernardo Dovizi da Bibbiena*, the acute *Portrait of Cardinal Inghirami*, the softly modelled *Madonna of the Baldachin* and the tender *Madonna of the Chair*; to be noted in particular in the **Jupiter Room** (ceiling by Pietro da Cortona, 1643-45) is the *Madonna del Sacco (Madonna of the Sack)* by Perugino, Andrea del Sarto's *St. John the Baptist*, the powerful and intense figure of *Saint Mark* by Fra Bartolomeo, the *Annunciation*, once more by Andrea del Sarto, the charming *Holy Family* by Rubens, and the enigmatic delicate *Portrait of a Woman*, known as *La Velata*, by Raphael. The **Mars Room** (ceiling by Pietro da Cortona, 1646) houses Murillo's *Madonna and Child* and *Madonna of the Rosary*, the famous *Consequences of War* by Rubens, the *Portrait of Daniele Barbaro*, a glowing painting by Veronese, Titian's *Portrait of Cardinal Ippolito de' Medici* and Van Dyck's *Cardinal Luigi*

Bentivoglio; to be noted in particular in the **Apollo Room** (ceiling by Pietro da Cortona, 1660) is Titian's sensuous *Magdalen*, the dramatic *Deposition* by Andrea del Sarto, the *Portrait of Vincenzo Zeno* by Tintoretto and Rosso Fiorentino's *Madonna Enthroned with Saints*. Particularly striking in the **Venus Room** (ceiling by Pietro da Cortona, 1641-42) is the *Portrait of a Woman*, known as *La Bella*, by Titian, his *Portrait of Pietro Aretino*, one of the outstanding achievements of the Renaissance, and the lively painting of *Ulysses Returning from the Island of Phaecia* by Rubens.

Galleria d'Arte Moderna (Piazza Pitti - Palazzo Pitti - Open: 9-14, holid. 9-13, closed Mondays.) Situated on the second floor of Palazzo Pitti, the Gallery of Modern Art has over 2000 works of sculpture and painting by artists who were active between the beginning of the 19th century up to the early decades of the 20th century. The Gallery consists of many rooms: the first of these contain works in neoclassic and Romantic style with imposing historical paintings; deserving of special mention are the prized *Bust of Napoleon* by Canova in **Room IV**, the large group of *Cain and Abel* by Duprè in **Room X**, various fine *portraits* by Antonio Ciseri in **Room XII**, and works by the great Giovanni Boldini in **Room XV**; *The Rain of Ashes* and *On the Banks of the Ofanto* by Giuseppe de Nitis in **Room XVII**. **Rooms XXIII and XXIV** contain a rich collection of works by the most important Macchiaioli painters: Silvestro Lega, Giuseppe Abbati, Telemaco Signorini, Cristiano Banti, Edoardo Borrani, Vincenzo Cabianca, Cesare Ciani to name only the best known. **Room XXIII** also contains some of the outstanding works by the father of the Macchiaioli movement, Giovanni Fattori.

Museo degli Argenti (Piazza Pitti - Palazzo Pitti - Open: 9-14, holid. 9-13, closed Mondays.) The Museum is comprised of various rooms overlooking the Courtyard of Bacchus. The first three rooms are decorated with allegorical and trompe-l'oeil frescoes by Michelangelo Colonna and Agostino Micheli. The frescoes in the fourth room consist of noteworthy allegories which exalt the *Deeds* of Lorenzo the Magnificent. The Museum contains examples of household and religious objects in precious metals, bowls and splendid vases in pietre dure and rock crystal as well as marvelous *ivories* and the vases from the collection of Lorenzo the Magnificent. Particularly striking is the famous *vase in lapis lazzuli* by Biliverto, next to the German ivories from the collection of Prince Mattia de' Medici. The treasure is exhibited in another room. It includes rare jewels and the «*Galanterie Gioiellate*» of Anna Maria Luisa Ludovica, the last of the Medicis. The small room on the mezzanine contains ceramics and porcelain.

Museo delle Porcellane (Porcelain Museum) - (Piazza Pitti - Boboli Gardens. Open: 9-14, holid. 9-13, closed Mondays.) This small Museum is in the Boboli Gardens in the Palazzina del Cavaliere and contains a collection of porcelain - Sevres, Chantilly, Vienna, Meissen, Worcester and other manufactories - some of which belonged to Elisa Baciocchi, Napoleon's sister.

Contini-Bonacossi Collection (Piazza Pitti - Boboli Gardens.) The collection was presented to the State in 1969 and is on exhibit in the **Meridiana**, a pavilion to the west of Palazzo Pitti. It is composed of fine *majolicas*, interesting *antiquities*, but above all important paintings including Cimabue's *Madonna and Saints*, Sassetta's *Madonna of the Snow*, the *portrait of Count Da Porto with his Son*, by Veronese, Goya's moving *Torero* and *El Aguador de Sevilla* by Velazquez.

Boboli Gardens The Boboli Gardens comprise the largest monumental green space in Florence. The history of the gardens goes back four centuries. In 1549 Cosimo I de' Medici commisioned them from Niccolo Pericoli, called Tribolo. After his death the undertaking was continued and added to by Ammannati, Buontalenti, and finally Alfonso Parigi the Younger.
Today entrance to the gardens is through the **Bacchus Courtyard** beyond which is the charming **Buontalenti Grotto** (1583), an artificial grotto consisting of various chambers covered with artificial incrustations and frescoes. The first chamber contains idyllic images by Poccetti and statues by Baccio Bandinelli; the second, known as **Nymphaeum** is lined with shells and decorated with mythological paintings; at the center is the fine sculptural group of *Paris and Helen* (1560) by Vincenzo de' Rossi, and a finely worked basin by Battista Lorenzi. The third chamber, completely decorated by Poccetti, contains a splendid *Fountain with Satyrs* who leer at the *Venus of the Grot-*

Palazzo Pitti: from the top left, the Fountain of Bacchus, *the* Fountain of Neptune *and the back of the palazzo*

ticella (1573) by Giambologna.

The fine alley flanked by Roman statues leads to the **Amphitheater** designed by Tribolo, at the center of which is a large Roman marble *basin* and an Egyptian *obelisk* from Thebes (2nd cent. B.C.). The two Roman statues of *Septimius Severus* and a *Magistrate* near the Amphitheater are particularly fine. Further up is a large basin called **Neptune's Pond** with at the center a fine bronze statue of Neptune by Stoldo Lorenzi (1565).

On the highest level, at the back of the park, we can admire the *Statue of Abundance*, begun by Giambologna and finished by Tacca (1636). Nearby are the old walls constructed by Michelangelo in 1529, near a bastion with the **Grand Duke's Casino** and the nearby **Giardino del Cavaliere** with the fine *Monkey fountain* by Pietro Tacca.

Further downhill is an annex of Palazzo Pitti called the **Meridiana**, a pleasant neo-Gothic building (1832). An alternative itinerary from Neptune's pond begins in a steep alley, known as the **Viottolone**, which leads to the **Piazzale dell'Isolotto**. Here, at the center of a charming garden is the stupendous *Oceanus Fountain* by Alfonso Parigi (1618), a copy with variations of Giambologna's figure of Neptune, surrounded by statues that symbolically represent the young *Nile*, the adult *Ganges* and the old *Euphrates*, the whole theatrically set up with other statues that emerge from the water such as *Perseus* and *Andromeda*.

Museo della Specola (Via Romana 17. Open: Tuesdays 9-12, Sundays 9-12. Wax Museum - Museo delle Cere - Open Saturdays 14-17.) Founded in 1775 by Grand Duke Pietro Leopoldo with scientific material inherited from the Medicis, the museum has important zoological, botanic, mineralogical collections and a fine group of scientific instruments. The museum is also famous for its collection of statues in colored wax which reproduce anatomical models, made in the 18th century by masters of the famous Florentine school of «*ceraioli*»; one of the most famous is the so-called «*flayed figure*» which reproduces the muscles and blood vessels of a human being. In the so-called «**Tribune of Galileo**», built by Giuseppe Martelli, are a cycle of *frescoes* by Giuseppe Bezzuoli, Nicola Cinafanelli, Gaspare Martellini and Luigi Sabatelli. The *statue of Galileo* is by Aristodemo Costoli.

Church of Santa Felicita On the site of an ancient oratory of the 5th century, the church has often been remodeled. Its present aspect is due to Federico Ruggeri (1736).

Under the **porch** are various *tombs* including that *of the merchant Barduccio Chierichini* (1416) and that *of cardinal Luigi De Rossi*, by Raffaele di Montelupo (1500).

The **interior** has a single nave and is in neoclassic style.

Various chapels open off the nave between the pilaster strips: the first chapel on the right was built for the Capponi family by Brunelleschi (1425); on the altar is a *Deposition* (1528), one of Pontomo's masterpieces. On the wall to the right is his famous *Annunciation*. In the pendentives are roundels of the *Four Evangelists* by Pontormo and Bronzino.

To the right of the transept is the **Sacristy** (1470) in the style of Brunelleschi and uncertain attribution (Michelozzo or Leon Battista Alberti). On the walls are an *Adoration of the Magi* by Francesco di Antonio (1450), a polyptych, *Madonna and Child with Saints*, by Taddeo Gaddi, and a *Saint Felicity with her Seven Sons* by Neri di Bicci. In the small apse a fine *Crucifix* by Pacino di Buonaguida, a 15th-century *Pietà* by an unknown painter and a *Madonna* by Giovanni del Biondo.

Church of Santo Spirito The church of Santo Spirito founded in 1250 received its present form in the 15th century when it was built after a model by Brunelleschi who had conceived it as a twin to the church of San Lorenzo. The **facade** however was never finished and is still only a rough plastered wall with an undefined silhouette at the top.

The fine **dome** was designed by Brunelleschi, while the soaring **bell tower** is by Baccio d'Agnolo (1503). The **interior** is one of the finest examples of Renaissance architecture, a Latin cross with three spacious aisles. The colonnade moves forward in a succession of light arches supported by 35 elegant Corinthian columns in *pietra serena*, forming what is no other than an internal portico. The ground plan of the 40 semicircular chapels repeats the semicircular rhythm of the arches.

The **internal facade** is comprised of three large doors and was made by

Church of Santo Spirito

Salvi d'Andrea (1483) on Brunelleschi's design. Behind the *high altar* is a *Crucifix* that may be an early work by Michelangelo. In the right crossing are various important examples of painting: in the third chapel the «*Madonna del Soccorso*» by an unknown 15th-century painter; in the fifth chapel, Filippino Lippi's famous *Madonna and Child with Saints*. Other fine works are in the left crossing; in the first chapel a *Madonna and Child with Angels and Saints* by Raffaellino del Garbo; in the second, *Saint Monica Establishing the Rule of the Augustinian Nuns* by Francesco Botticini; in the third, a delicate *Madonna and Child with Saints* by Cosimo Rosselli and, in the fourth, a marble *altar* by Andrea Sansovino. Other important works are also in the apse chapels: in the first is the *Madonna with Saints* by Lorenzo di Credi; in the third the *Madonna and Child with Four Saints* by Maso di Banco.

Entry to the **Vestibule** and the **Sacristy** is near the organ. The former is by Andrea Sansovino and the latter has a fine octagonal ground plan by Giuliano da Sangallo and Cronaca (1456).

The vestibule leads to the **First Cloister** in 17th-century style with frescoes of the same period. From here to the **Second Cloister**, built by Ammannati and frescoed by Poccetti (the cloister is not at present open to the public since it is occupied by the recruiting center).

Entry to the nearby **Refectory** is from the piazza. It contains the imposing fresco of the *Last Supper* by Nardo di Cione.

Church of Santa Maria del Carmine The 14th-century building was almost completely destroyed in a fire in 1771. The present structure is therefore 18th century and was built by G. Ruggeri and G. Mannaioni on a Latin cross plan with a single aisle. The works inside include Vasari's *Crucifixion* on the third altar to the right.

One of the greatest works of the entire Renaissance came through the fire miraculously intact - the **Brancacci Chapel** in the right transept which preserves a cycle of extremely important frescoes which have recently been restored. The frescoes were begun in 1425 by Masolino da Panicale, who painted the *Temptation of Adam and Eve* in the first compartment above right; *St. Peter Resuscitating Tabitha* in the first scene to the right of the large compartment at the top; and the *Preaching of St. Peter* above, to the left of the altar. The compartment on the right wall, *St. Peter Heals a Cripple*, is in part by the great Masaccio who also painted the compartment above to the right of the altar with *St. Peter Baptizing the Neophytes* and the splendid *Expulsion from Paradise* in the first panel above left. Masaccio then went on to the large compartment at the top of the left wall, with the scenes of the *Tribute Money - St. Peter taking the Coin from the Mouth of the Fish* (left), *Jesus Ordering Peter to Fish* (center), and *St. Peter paying the Tribute to the Publican* (right). In the lower tier the compartment to the right of the altar with *St. Peter and St. John distributing the Goods* and the *Death of Ananias* is by Masaccio as are also, to the left of the altar, *St. Peter Healing the Sick*

Church of the Carmine: detail of the Tribute Money,
restored fresco by Masaccio

with his Shadow; on the lower part of the left wall, *St. Peter in Cattedra* (left)
and part of *St. Peter Bringing back to Life the Son of the Prefect Theophilus
of Antioch*. Finally the last compartment of the left wall, *St. Peter in Prison
Visited by St. Paul*, in the lower zone of the right wall, the *Angel Freeing
St. Peter from Prison* and the double scene of *St. Peter before the Prefect
Agrippa* and the *Crucifixion of St. Peter* are by another great artist, Filippino
Lippi.

Church of the Carmine: detail of the Resurrection of Tabitha,
restored fresco by Masolino

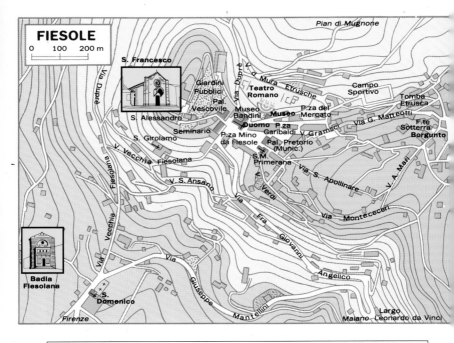

FIESOLE

Church of San Domenico - Badia Fiesolana - **Duomo** - Piazza Mino
da Fiesole - Sant'Alessandro - **Convent of San Francesco** - Museo
Bandini

Historical survey. Numerous finds of the Etruscan civilization have come
to light in the vast zone to the north of the Arno between the Sieve and
Ombrone rivers. The so-called «Fiesole stelae» date back as far as the late
6th century B.C. However finds from the Villanovan culture of the early iron
age and the age of copper and of bronze have also been unearthed. The
Etruscan settlement of Fiesole was probably the center of a zone where set-
tlements were scattered over the hillsides which overlook the Florentine basin. Remains from this period include various stretches of the powerful *city
wall* and the ruins of a *Temple* with two wings and two columns in the pro-
naos. Since some of the walls are still intact it can be considered as one of
the most important examples of this kind in all of Etruria. A considerable
number of interesting finds from the Etruscan period - urns, bucchero, clay
and bronze statues - together with other objects from Roman times are to
be found in the *Museum* near the archaeological zone. Invaded by the Gauls
in 225 B.C. and captured by Marcus Porcius Cato in 90 B.C., it was occupied
by Silla in 80 B.C. and turned into a military colony. This was when Fiesole
became a Roman city (*Faesulae*) with a forum, temples, theater, baths. The
Theater, which is still well preserved, is sometimes used for spectacles of
classic theater and has a capacity of about 3,000 people. It dates to the beginning of the imperial age and was improved in the period of Claudius and of
Septimius Severus. The *Baths* too belong to the early empire and were
remodelled by Hadrian.
In republican times (1st cent. B.C.) the *Temple*, originally Etruscan, was
rebuilt. An explanation for the prosperity of Etruscan and Roman Fiesole is
to be found in its fortunate geographical site near a ford over the Arno - close
to where *Florentia* was to rise. The territory of the Roman *Municipium* of
Fiesole must have extended prevalently to the north of the Arno while the
territory of the «*colonia*» of Florence must have lain above all to the south
of the river. Occupied by the Ostrogoths and the Byzantines, Fiesole from
the 6th century on was the site of a Lombard settlement as documented by
the remains of a necropolis. In 1125, after military campaigns, Florence
wiped out the city forcing it into submission and destroying part of the
centuries-old city walls.

Church of San Domenico The roads that lead from Florence to the hill of Fiesole all converge on the plateau where the church of San Domenico stands, annexed to the convent which was founded in 1406. The Renaissance layout of the building was transformed between the end of the 16th and the beginning of the 17th century by Dosio (tribune and choir) and Matteo Nigetti (porch on the facade and bell tower). The complex contains a wealth of works of art: outstanding are various *paintings* by Fra Angelico, who sojourned in the convent. Saint Antonine, Bishop of Florence in the first half of the 15th century, also stayed there, and that Fra Domenico Buonvicini who was burned at the stake with Savonarola in 1498.

Badia Fiesolana The Badia Fiesolana stands on the site of the old cathedral of Fiesole dedicated to Saint Peter, on the steep road that climbs to San Domenico from the Ponte alla Badia on the Via Faentina.
The Camaldoli friars replaced the original church with one of which the Romanesque **facade** decorated in dark green and white marble like San Miniato al Monte remains. The monastery (12th cent.) passed to the Benedictine order which kept it until 1439 when it was transferred to the Augustinian canons of the congregation of San Frediano of Lucca and then finally to the Scolopi.
From the middle of the 15th century on, thanks to the munificence and desire of Cosimo the Elder, the church and much of the complex were renewed. The religious building is now an example of early Renaissance architecture. It is a Latin cross plan, with barrel vaulting and side chapels. The whitewashed surfaces are clearly articulated by molding in *pietra serena*. Cosimo himself lived in the **Convent**, which has an elegant **Cloister**. He had quarters built for himself and collected rare codexes which after the suppression of the goods of the church in 1778, passed to the Biblioteca Laurenziana. It must also be recalled that in 1753 the Accademia dei Georgofili was instituted here, the first of an agrarian nature in Europe.

Cathedral Fiesole, set between the two hills of San Francesco and Sant'Apollinare, is at present one of the most famous places in the environs of Florence. Outstanding among the city's monuments is the cathedral dedicated to S. Romolo. Begun in the 11th century, it was later completed and enlarged, then remodeled and restored and integrated at the end of the 19th century, especially in the facade and the tower. The **interior** is on a basilica plan, with a nave divided from the side aisles by round piers - some with reused Roman capitals - and with a large semi-circular apse. A large **crypt** lies under the choir which is therefore raised above the floor level of the aisles, as is the case in the basilica of San Miniato al Monte near Florence.

The hill of Fiesole

Piazza Mino da Fiesole

Piazza Mino da Fiesole To the left of the cathedral is the ***Rectory***, originally 11th- century but rebuilt in the first half of the 15th century. The same may be said for the ***Palazzo Vescovile*** or ***Bishop's Palace*** which was begun in the same period but finished in the late 17th century, the date of the neighboring ***Seminary*** as well. The ***Palazzo Pretorio*** stands on a slight elevation on the eastern side of the large square which is named after Mino da Fiesole. The Palazzo is a picturesque structure prevalently 15th- century in style, preceded by a light architraved porch. The small church of ***Santa Maria Primerana***, with a 16th-century porch in front, closes off the square on the east together with the Palazzo Pretorio.

Sant'Alessandro The ancient basilica of Sant'Alessandro lies almost at the top of the steep road that leads to the top of the hill of San Francesco. Originally this was the site of an Etruscan temple, then replaced by a Roman temple and then by the Christian church, the origins of which are said to go back to S. Theodoric, and which may have inherited the capitals and columns of the Roman building. Almost certainly of pre-Romanesque origins, the church was renewed in the 11th century, then remodelled in the 16th and 18th centuries with the addition of a neoclassic facade at the beginning of the 19th century. Recent restoration has once more brought to light the Romanesque structures. The columns in oriental cipolin marble with Ionic capitals and bases are particularly noteworthy.

The Convent of San Francesco The Convent of San Francesco now stands on the top of the hill that was once the site of the Etruscan acropolis and then of the Roman acropolis, followed by the medieval fortress which was destroyed by the Florentines in 1125. Founded at the beginning of the 14th century as the headquartes of the Florentine hermits, it was turned over to the Franciscans in the early 15th century. They enlarged the ***Church*** - which now consists of a long narrow nave with barrel vaulting - and the ***Convent***, of which San Bernardino of Siena was abbot.

Museo Bandini Fiesole also has a picture gallery with numerous *paintings*, above all Florentine painting of the 14th-15th centuries, collected in the late 18th century by the canon Angiolo Maria Bandini - after whom the museum is named - who left them as legacy to the Chapter of Fiesole.

Church of San Francesco and Roman theater.

INDEX

© Copyright by CASA EDITRICE BONECHI, Via Cairoli, 18/b Florence - Italy
Tel. 055/576841 - Fax 055/5000766 E-mail: bonechi@bonechi.it Internet: www.bonechi.it
*Team work. All rights reserved. No part of this publication may be reproduced or
transmitted in any form or by any means, electronic, chemical or mechanical, including
photocopying, recording, or by any information storage and retrieval system, without
permission in writing from the publisher. The cover, layout and artwork by the* Casa
Editrice Bonechi *graphic artists in this publication are protected by international copyright.*
Translated by Erika Pauli *for* Studio Comunicare, Florence.
Printed in Italy by Centro Stampa Editoriale Bonechi.
Photographs from the Archives of Casa Editrice Bonechi.
ISBN 88-7009-438-3
* * *